RUNNING
JUMPING
THROWING
FOR YOUTH

RUNNING
JUMPING
THROWING
FOR YOUTH

FUNDAMENTAL TECHNIQUES
AND TRAINING ROUTINES
IN TRACK AND FIELD

Written by
Wolfgang Lohmann, PhD

Edited by
Peter Klavora, PhD
Faculty of Physical Education
and Health
University of Toronto

Sport Books Publisher

Translation by Linda Paul

Canadian Cataloguing in Publication Data

Lohmann, Wolfgang
    Running, jumping, throwing for youth

1st Canadian ed.
Translation of: Lauf-Sprung-Wurf.
ISBN 0-920905-32-3

1. Track-athletics – Training. I. Klavora, Peter.
II. Title.

GV1060.675.T73L6413 1990 796.4'2 C89-094510-1

Distribution worldwide by
Sport Books Publisher
278 Robert Street
Toronto, ON M5S 2K8

Fax: 416-966-9022
E-mail: sbp@sportbookspub.com
Web: http://www.sportbookspub.com

Printed in Canada

Contents

Foreword

You've all heard of the budding young track star who is spectacular in one sport, but whose grades in P.E. class always seem to be low. The main reason is that health depends on all-around physical development, and proficiency in one sport only can be detrimental to the development of good general health and physical well-being. The student who shows ability in a wide range of activities brings home the best P.E. grades.

All-round training is also the most reliable foundation for achieving a high level of performance in a specialized field, e.g., track and field, tennis, basketball, soccer, etc. This foundation is acquired the most quickly and effectively in childhood and adolescence.

It pays to begin with a varied training program even if your ultimate goal is to specialize in one particular event. Such a program might include activities as diverse as gymnastics, swimming, handball, soccer, and basketball. Similarly, even if you have decided to specialize in a single track event, such as high jumping or discus throwing, your training program should embrace a wide variety of other track and field activities as well.

This book contains a wide variety of exercises for the track and field athlete that can be done individually, in small groups, and with or without the assistance of your coach or P.E. teacher. Of course, you are encouraged to ask for advice from others—your P.E. teacher, your coach and even your parents. Whatever approach you feel comfortable with, if you combine the independent practice exercises contained in this book with formal training in track and field, we are confident that you will find the book extremely beneficial.

Editor

About Training

Training and Health

It's easy to get caught up in a training program, especially if it is producing results. But there is always the tendency to go a little too quickly, and to follow your program in a way that may be harmful to your health. To get the most out of your training program — and to promote good health — we suggest that you observe the following guidelines:

1. Get regular medical check-ups, and show the doctor your training program.

2. Those of you who cannot participate fully in physical education classes for medical reasons should stick to exercises that your doctor has recommended.

3. Colds are a strain on the heart. If you have a cold or flu, you should not train. Wait a week after you have recovered and then gradually start training again.

4. Avoid colds by showering in warm water — and then in cold water — immediately following your training.

5. To achieve results, every training session must be strenuous. You will not overstrain if you follow our approximate figures for exercise repetitions. To be on the safe side, check with your physical education teacher before increasing your training.

6. A stitch in the side usually indicates that you have attempted too much. Take a short break and breathe deeply.

Training Throughout the Year

Once you have decided to begin training, you must have a regular schedule. You must know how to set up your training program. To have enough time to prepare for summer competitions, track and field athletes begin their training year in the fall or, at the latest, in the winter. If you're just starting your training, don't worry about adapting yourself to the season. Start now.

Naturally, you must wear warm clothing in rainy or cold weather. In spring and summer, however, just wear a T-shirt and gym shorts under your track suit. When it's very warm, take-off your track suit after warming up. In cooler weather you'll take longer to warm-up than in the summer months. The best time to train in the fall and winter is early afternoon at the warmest part of the day. As the temperature rises and the days lengthen in the spring, you can move your training to later in the afternoon.

Speed and strength are the basis for track and field athletic technique. You should concentrate on these. But during the winter months, you should give high priority to endurance training, mostly through running.

A Week's Training Schedule

Initially two training sessions per week are enough. Those who wish to achieve good performance quickly must, of course, work up to five sessions per week, but gradually.

The exercises should be combined in the following way: short distance with high jump; and long jump with throwing practice.

Each training session can be finished with endurance running. For best results, you should alternate the events so that each has priority at specific times in the program as shown below:

Legend:

E   endurance running
S   sprinting
L   long jump
H   high jump
R   rounders* and club throwing
SP shot put

* A game of English origin that is played with ball and bat. It resembles baseball

Note: less time should be devoted to exercises denoted in low case.

A Sample of Rick's (14-year-old) Weekly Training Schedule

Time pm.	Monday	Tuesday	Wednesday	Thursday	Friday	Saturday	Sunday
2:00–3:00	afternoon rest	afternoon helping with housework		long school day	afternoon rest	help with housework	free time
3:00–4:00	homework	homework	homework	rest	homework	homework	training T+S e
4:00–5:00	training L+SP	circuit training 3X	free time	homework	training H+S	free time	afternoon free time
5:00–6:00	e	free time	training H+S	help with housework	E	circuit training 4X	
6:00–7:00	homework	free time	e		homework and free time	free time	

Points to Remember before a Competition

1. It is especially important to train regularly several weeks before a sports meet.

2. During this time, strength and speed exercises should be given priority

3. If you are not participating in a multi-event competition, then you should focus on your main event.

4. Do not train as extensively the week before; instead concentrate on building up your strength. Make sure you do not exert yourself too much in one area. Do general strength exercises and balance games.

A Day's Training Schedule

An hour of training includes
(1) the warm-up,
(2) track and field exercises, and
(3) body care.
The table below shows how an hour of training is set up. The warm-up exercises are described on the following pages, and the track and field exercises may be found in later chapters.

A few words about body care: anyone who exercises properly sweats. As a result certain bacteria settle on your skin along with particles of dust and dirt. In other words, you are dirty after exercising. Athletes should wash themselves after every training session and change their clothes. Rinsing in cold water toughens your skin and protects you in this way from colds and other infections.

A Sample Plan for One Hour Training Session

Part of Training	Time (min.)	Exercises	Page In Book
Warm-up	10	5 min. endurance run 2 Domino circuit, exercises 1 and 8 from each page	
Main Part S H Conclusion ℓ	20 20 10	• S3, S4, – 2 sets each of ex. 1 • H1, ex. 3; ex. 4, 2 sets each • endurance run	
Body care	15-20	trot home, wash, change clothes	

Exercise in Sets

All exercises are practised in sets. By sets, we mean the repetition of the same exercise several times with only short breaks or no breaks in between.

Only after a certain number of repetitions should you break. The breaks can be of varying lengths and in track and field exercises, from 2 to 3 minutes long. They are followed by the next set of the same or different exercises. Each training session should include 2 to 3 sets of 4 to 6 different exercises.

11

A Few Words about the Warm-up

Warming or limbering up before each training session and especially before competition is necessary for two reasons.

1. The muscles in your body have to accomplish more during athletic activity. To do this, they need more nutrients and more oxygen, both of which they get by using more blood. The body has reserves in the abdominal organs for this purpose. The moderate use of strength during warm-up exercises allows the organism to tap into the these reserves.

   The heart must also work harder to circulate the larger quantity of blood. The lungs breathe more deeply and quickly to make more oxygen available. In warm-up, the organs are prepared in all these ways for the greater effort that they will be required to expend. Again, the key word here is gradual. Gradually working up to a certain level of exercise is always more effective in the long run than leaping right in to a demanding exercise routine.

2. Our muscles are like a motor— as long as they are cold, they do not work to full potential. Our limbs are normally cooler than our bodies. We therefore warm them up with some preparatory exercises.

   The following program is suitable:
   - warming-up by doing a slow endurance run, 600 to 800 m;
   - doing a circuit that includes general strengthening exercises for the arm, trunk, and leg muscles.

On the next few pages we present a number of these exercises. At the bottom of this page are the symbols that show the purpose of each exercise. On page 16 we explain how an organized circuit program can be developed using a game of dominoes!

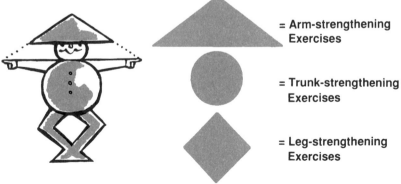

= **Arm-strengthening Exercises**

= **Trunk-strengthening Exercises**

= **Leg-strengthening Exercises**

1. Shoot up from the ground like a spring—stretch jump.
2. Stretch jump in a squat position.
3. Stretch jump keeping heels high.
4. Long kangaroo hops forward.
5. Duck walk.
6. Bunny hops.
7. Knee bends.
8. Knee bends on one leg.
9. Jump up and down steps from a standing position.
10. Run up and down steps.
11. Half knee bends in pairs.
12. In a half knee bend, straighten up against the tightly stretched expander while counting to six. During the count gradually increase the intensity, then hold maximal effort for 2 seconds, slowly let go. Rest approximately 1 minute.

1. Tense the body like a bow with feet anchored.
2. Who can rock the highest?
3. Arch yourself as high as possible.
4. Stretch your body into a bridge without using your arms.
5. Pick up a glass with your teeth and hold it for 3 or 4 seconds.
6. Pull backward against a tight rope, count to six.
7. Sit-ups.
8. Rapid javelin-knifes.
9. Making circles with your feet.
10. Lift legs to horizontal position.
11. Swing your leg over your head in one smooth motion.
12. Lift and lower tensed legs quickly.

14

1. Push-ups.
2. Push-ups with feet raised.
3. Who can throw a heavy stone the farthest?
4. Standing push-ups off a wall with feet as far back as possible.
5. Pull-ups from a horizontal position.
6. Chin-ups from a stretched hang.
7. Rope climbing.
8. Lifting a shot with straight arms.
9. Pushing against a door frame.
10. One-arm pulls on an exerciser cable.
11. Pushing the stool together.
12. One-arm pulls with both arms on exercise expander.
    Exercises 9 to 12 are isometric strengthening exercises; strength is used as in exercise 12, page 13.

15

From Dominoes to Circuit Training

You all know the game of dominoes. In dominoes, pieces with the same numbers, points, or symbols are placed together. You can invent a similar game yourselves, but using strengthening exercises instead of points. On p. 141 and 143, you will find squares prepared for you to cut out for the domino exercise. When they are played, the same symbols must always be placed together. The result is an exercise order similar to that of circuit training, one that can be repeated over and over again. The leg, back, abdomen, and arm muscles will be alternated. At least four exercises are needed to make up a circuit, but you can put as many as 8 together. To do this, you will need more domino cards. You can make these following the pattern on p. 141 with numbers corresponding to each exercise group shown on the previous pages. On the left is the symbol for the exercise illustrated, and on the right, the symbol for the exercise to follow. Compare with our examples. You can easily make up many circuit training variations.

Methods for circuit training

Method A: The number of repetitions of each exercise should follow our instructions. Begin with two complete circuits and try every week to do the same circuit one additional time. When you have reached six circuits, go back to two, but increase the number of repetitions of each exercise to three.

Method B: Time yourselves. Each time try to reduce the time needed to complete each circuit.

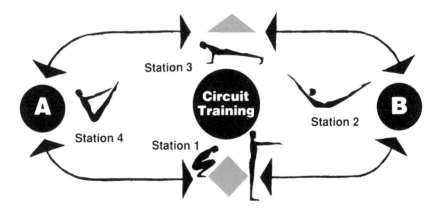

Station 3
Circuit Training
A
B
Station 2
Station 4
Station 1

Endurance Running

Nothing Works without Endurance

Athletes often say, "I'm a sprinter (jumper, thrower). I only need strength and speed for that, so I don't include endurance runs in my training program."

By omitting them, however, they are making a big mistake. Each training session makes certain demands on the circulation system and, as a result, on endurance. So the better your endurance the better your circulation and ultimately your strength. In short, the better your heart the harder and more effectively the body can work at training.

In general, a better-than-average circulatory system is a fundamental requirement for a healthy and robust person. If you are young, you have an extra advantage: the growing body adapts quickly as the heart becomes stronger and the lungs are able to take in more oxygen. Endurance running, then, is indispensable to your training program. But don't let yourself be tempted into too much endurance development, even if you discover that long runs are especially enjoyable. Too much distance running can lower the development of running speed. Since this can seldom be developed when you are older, you should avoid too much endurance running.

Looking for a Running Route

Where Should You Run?

It is better to run on paths through woods and parks where there is an abundance of foliage. Why? Not because it is prettier to look at, although this may be true. Rather, the oxygen content of the air tends to be elevated in these areas (since the leaves of plants produce oxygen). If there are no paths in your area, run on the side streets to avoid traffic, and avoid intersections where possible. An important factor to consider is that the start and finish of your route is not too far from where you live, since you will be overheated and completely soaked in sweat. This is the time when the danger of catching a cold is greatest, especially in cool weather. You should get home quickly.

The route does not need to be completely level: climbing hills is good for you, but avoid long or steep hills.

Where possible, train where there are not too many people watching or getting in the way. Young athletes must learn to practise on their own. If you train without an "audience," you will find that you will do that much better in competition when the audience is there to stimulate you.

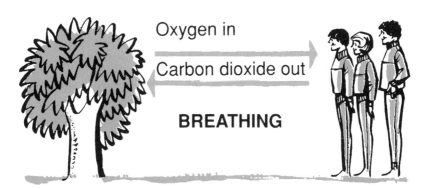

Oxygen in

Carbon dioxide out

BREATHING

How Long Should the Route Be?

The route should be laid out so that it can be lengthened at any time. With regular training, you will soon be able to run several kilometers. At first it is best to run a straight stretch (to the turning point and back) that can be turned into a complete circuit later. Start to finish should be approximately 2000 m. The circuit should be 2000 to 4000 m long. Variations are possible according to individual needs.

How to Measure the Route?

You need a bicycle. Tie a piece of red or white string on the valve of the front wheel. Then set the string on a mark on the ground and push the bicycle forward until the string touches the ground again. Make another mark on this spot. The distance between the two marks is the distance the wheel covers in one revolution. Now push the bicycle over the running route, count the number of revolutions the marked wheel makes and calculate:

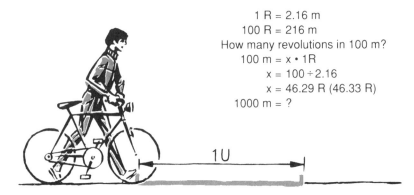

$$1\ R = 2.16\ m$$
$$100\ R = 216\ m$$
How many revolutions in 100 m?
$$100\ m = x \cdot 1R$$
$$x = 100 \div 2.16$$
$$x = 46.29\ R\ (46.33\ R)$$
$$1000\ m = ?$$

1 U

Do the calculation using the length of one revolution of your tire. Here is the formula once more. When measured, the length of one revolution of our bicycle wheel was 2.16 m. One hundred revolutions are then 216 m. But we would like to know where each 100 m mark is. Therefore we must calculate how many revolutions our tire makes in 100 m. To do this, we divide 100 by the length of our tire's revolution. We find that 46 1/3 revolutions make 100 m. 1000 m is ten times as much, thus 463 revolutions. Mark off every 100 m.

Make a sketch of your route. This is a practical measure so that you do not forget its layout. In addition, it enables you to determine after running how much of the route you have covered. You need this information to organize a training plan.

Have a clear picture of the route in your head, something like the one shown in the illustration below. All landmarks and bends in the route should be noted. Then sketch the course as if you were hovering over it in a helicopter and looking directly down on it. Draw the roads and landmarks using these symbols:

houses

deciduous
   forest

body of water

church

meadow

restaurant

look-out point

coniferous
   forest

railway tracks

bridge

path

Running Training Begins

First develop the ability to run for a longer time using moderate exertion, without tiring yourself out. We suggest that you work towards this goal in two stages.

Training Rules for the First Stage

1. Begin by running only for a set length of time, without thinking about distance. Start with 5 minutes. If you find that easy, increase to 6 minutes the next time. Increase the time only when you find the previous time has become easy.

2. Maintain an even pace by turning around when exactly half the time is up and running back in the same time used for the first part. If your initial pace was too fast, you will run a slower second half because of fatigue. Your pace is right if you can run 1 km in 5:00 to 5:30 minutes. That is 3 to 3.3 m per second (m/s).

3. This stage is over when you can run the entire stretch in the determined length of time and maintain the right time without a stopwatch.

Training Rules for the Second Stage

1. The training route is now the circular one.

2. The goal is to increase distance while maintaining an even speed.

3. When running farther becomes difficult, use will power. Set yourself a goal of another 100 to 200 m, and stop only when that goal is achieved.

4. After the run, do not just stand around. Definitely do not sit down: that can be harmful. Keep moving while breathing deeply. Take the shortest route home.

5. At home calculate your average speed by dividing the distance run by the running time. Example: 3500 m : 1110 s = 3.15 m/s. Always record the result in your exercise book.

6. You should not run more than 4 or 5 km. You won't need it for competition. Even those who wish to become intermediate or long distance runners must have all-round training first. Take up specific training as a teenager.

A Few Rules of Running Technique

With endurance running, you can control your technique because your pace is not fast. Pay attention to the following:

1. The strides should save your strength. They are therefore shorter than in a faster run. Avoid jerky movements; soft fluid strides work better. Try to relax muscles that are not working.

2. After the relatively short stage when you are airborne, land on the outside of the heel to encourage forward movement. Do not push too hard against the running direction when you land.

3. Keep your trunk in as close to vertical as possible.

4. Arms swing in rhythm to the run. They should swing either exactly in rhythm, or somewhat off with the hands close to the middle of the body.

5. Your breathing adapts itself to the rhythm. All runners must find their own rhythm. Breathe deeply through the mouth.

6. Keep your body relaxed.

Other Possibilities for Endurance Training

If there is enough snow in winter, put on your skis and ski the route. Of course, you must also learn the diagonal stride of the cross-country skier.

If you have a bicycle, encourage your parents to take you on extended bicycle trips on weekends. Bicycling is another way to promote endurance and is healthy for all age groups. In hot summer weather go swimming, but do not just splash around on the air mattress to cool off. Instead, try swimming a long distance as fast as possible. In a pond, lake, or pool without regular lanes, count your strokes. The next time you swim, try to increase the number.

In rainy weather you can run continuously up and down the stairs of your house at an easy pace and only on tiptoes. Be quiet, though, so that you do not disturb anyone. Knee bends performed rapidly until you are tired can also serve as a substitute. You must, however, repeat the exercise at least twice after a five-minute break.

Sprinting

Speed is the Key

Everyone knows that speed is by far the most important factor in short-distance running. But is it important only in sprinting? No. In fact it plays an important part in all track and field events.

It is often said that you must be born with speed and that it cannot be acquired through training. If this were so, only naturally talented people would be successful in track and field. We asked one world record holder for her opinion about speed and its development. This is what she said:

"It's true of course that training for speed is not as easy, for example, as training for endurance. An adult must already have certain speed qualities to be successful in sprint training. This is why people assume that one must be born a sprinter. My view is different: the basis for speed does not develop equally, independent of a person's age. Instead, it seems to develop best during childhood. As a child I often enjoyed running very fast. So I'd like to recommend the following:

1. Speed exercises belong in every training session, no matter which event you enjoy practising the most.

2. Make an effort, above all, to get going quickly at the start and to maintain that speed.

3. Learn to relax while sprinting. Only then can you be fast."

Techniques of the Crouch Start and the Sprint

A Few Words about Starting Blocks

Before the start, all runners should adjust their starting blocks to find the best possible starting position.

Remember:

1. The block with the flatter slope is for the front foot, the steeper for the back.

2. The first block should be positioned in 1 1/2 to 2 foot lengths behind the starting line. The second block is approximately another foot length back from the corner of the first block. In addition, it is set the width of one foot to the left or right, depending on which foot is behind.

3. The blocks must be set up to follow the running direction exactly.

4. The blocks must be firmly secured to prevent injury.

Making Your Own Starting Blocks

To practise the crouch start, you must have starting blocks. You can make your own from a block of wood 40 to 50 cm in length and 20 cm in diameter. Saw the block of wood in half on a slant and cut the ends off, also on an angle. Measure the angle beforehand so that the angle of the rear starting block is more acute than that of the forward block. Use nails or spikes to secure the block to the ground, as illustrated..

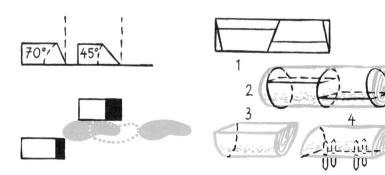

"On your mark!"

Pay Attention and You Will Learn Faster

First cover up the description of the exercise on the right hand side above.

Now look at the picture on the left and try to describe it in your own words. Begin with the legs or arms, but do not forget the head and trunk. Now: what does it say on the right side? Compare it with your description.

Below are pictures of mistakes. Try to name them. Then you will be able to recognize them in yourself and your friends.

The table that follows will help you learn to overcome them.

M1

What is Peter doing wrong?

His head ....

His eyes ....

His back ....

(Write it down for Peter.) Tell him also that with this starting position he is tensing his muscles improperly.

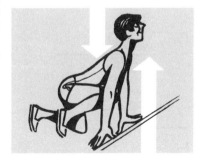

Remember These Instructions

- Step up to the starting blocks, crouch down, and place your feet firmly against the starting blocks.

- Hands are just behind the starting line, shoulder-width apart. Thumbs are extended and the backs of the hands point toward the finish line.

- Arms are straight and over the hands.

- Body weight is balanced between the hands and the knee.

- Back is slightly arched.

- Head is extended and eyes are on the starting line.

- When you have assumed the correct position, wait without moving and concentrate on the "get set" of the starter.

M2

Steven is concentrating, but:
His arms ....
His body weight ....
This position requires too much effort. It is almost like a push-up. Pushing off will be too hesitant.

M3

David is relaxed, but:
His body weight ....
His arms ....
Since he is almost sitting on his heels, it is hard for him to take the proper starting position on "get set."

"Set"

M4

Eric is concentrating improperly because:
His head ....
His back ....
He is already extending his back muscles. In most cases, he will straighten up too soon. (Compare with mistake 11.)

M5

Explain Paul's mistake:
His knees ....
His buttocks ....
His arms ....
Which other mistake is usually the cause for this? Look on page 29. Demonstrate how it should really look.

Remember What to Do on "Get Set"

- The back knee is lifted from the ground, bringing the buttocks up, not too slowly but not too jerkily.

- The starting position is correct when the front legs form almost a right angle at the knee. Buttocks are usually a little higher than the shoulders. The line of the back slopes from the head.

- Head remains lowered as in "on your mark."

- Body weight is evenly balanced between the four supports: hands and feet. The change of weight can be felt, especially in the hands.

- All senses are focused on the firing of the gun, in order to be able to take-off at lightning speed with all available strength.

M6

Jeffrey wants to take-off fast, but:
His buttocks ....
His knees ....
In this position, the first stride can never be quick since the knees are already almost straight.

M7

The leg position is good, but:
His arms. ....
His body weight. ....
Under this strain, the arms and shoulders stiffen, hindering a quick start.

"Go!"

M8

Susan's body is properly extended, but:
Her back foot ....
Her thigh ....
Before she takes her first stride, her competitors are already off.

M9

Michael works with his legs, but:
His front leg ....
His posture ....
His first stride will be long; it takes too long and he will fall behind.

Important Points at the Starter's Command

- Concentrate on getting all your strength ready for the start. It is at this instant that the race begins, and not after the first stride.

- The body rapidly extends itself forward and upward.

- The back foot, which takes the first stride, tries to make ground contact as quickly as possible to speed up the body.

- The hands push off only slightly from the ground. The arms swing alternately in short quick movements. Concentrate not only on the first arm swing, but also on the swing back, to encourage a quick second stride.

- Keep eyes on the track.

- This position is limited to the first 6 to 8 strides.

M10

Nick's extension is good, but:
His arms ....
His front leg ....
His rhythm is off and he cannot develop the speed that he is capable of.

M11

What is Martin doing wrong here?
His arms ....
His eyes ....
His back ....
What other mistakes can these weaknesses lead to?
Write them down. ....

Illustrated Summary Table of Mistakes

Mistake	Illustration

Brief description of mistakes

M1   Head held improperly because eyes are on the finish line—hollow back posture.

M2   Arms not extended—the center of gravity is too low.

M3   Arms are not vertical—the weight is too far back.

M4   Head is held improperly as in M1—hollow back posture.

M5   Sits too far back, the buttocks too low, the arms support on an angle.

M6   Buttocks are too high—the legs are almost straight.

M7   Leans too much on arms, which are not vertical.

M8   Already upright before the legs have made their first move.

M9   The swinging leg is too high.

M10   Both arms swing back.

Correction of Mistakes and Choice of Exercises

Correction	Exercises
Brief explanation how to correct mistakes	G: general hints S: specific exercises in book
Concentrate on the proper head position.	G: — S: S4, exercise 3.
Pay attention to the position of the arms.	G: — S: S4, exercise 3 from crouch start.
Balance your weight properly, pay attention to the arm position.	G: — S: S4, all exercises.
Look at the ground instead of starting out watching the finish line.	G: — S: S2, S4, all exercises.
Practice proper posture in front of the mirror.	G: — S: S4, exercise 3 from crouch start.
Pay attention to the arm position.	G: — S: S4, exercise 3.
Power in the legs and reaction ability lacking.	G: 1 to 4, 10 to 12, p. 13. S: S1, S2, all exercises; S4, exercise 3.
Do not concentrate on the start, concentrate on the ground.	G: — S: S4, all exercises.
Put hand corresponding to the front block somewhat forward.	G: — S: S4, exercises 2 and 3 from crouch start.

M1

Compare this runner with the first figure above. What is he doing wrong?

His head ....

His upper body ....

The result is that his legs are not extended far enough forward.

M2

What do you notice about Philip? Tell him his mistakes.

His feet ....

His upper body ....

His arms ....

Because of this, he is not running economically, as he does not move in a straight line to finish.

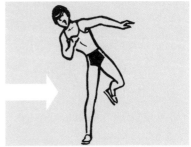

Running on a Track

When running on an track it is important that you follow the following points:

● Touch the ground with the balls of your feet. Run as if the ground were hot.

● Set your feet down one after the other as if on a line. The race is run in a straight line.

● Long fast strides come from putting your feet down firmly, right to the toes, from a high swinging leg.

● The arms swing rhythmically in the direction you are running, not at an angle of across the body. The elbows remain bent at the same angle.

● Do not clench your hands into fists.

● The body leans slightly forward without bending at the hips.

● Do not clench your jaw, leave your mouth relaxed.

M3

Susan leans forward, but:
Her hips ....
Her upper body ....
Her arms ....
She cannot make long strides and does not use all her muscles for a forward motion.

M4

Jean could run faster, since:
Her upper body ....
Her hips ....
She loses the use of part of her strength with every stride, because she is not totally extended. Each stride will be a little shorter.

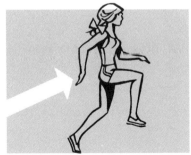

Illustrated Summary Table of Mistakes

Mistake	Illustration

Mistake   **Illustration**

M1   Head position—hollow back posture.

M2   Does not run in a straight line; upper body waddles like a duck; the arms swing across the body.

M3   Hips are not extended, upper body is too far forward.

M4   Upper body is too upright, hips are not extended, "sitting run!"

M5   Runs on whole foot.

M6   Runs with feet too far apart. The feet are not in a straight line.

M7   Feet are too far apart, toes are pointed out.

Correction of Mistakes and Choice of Exercises

Correction	Exercise
Head steers the body. Always practise proper head position when running.	G: Exercise 4 and 5, p 13. S: S1 and S3, all exercises.
Control arm and shoulder movements. They must follow the running direction.	G: — S: S2, exercise 4; S3 and S4, all exercises.
Learn the proper posture for your whole body. Think tall.	G: Exercise 4, p. 13. S: S2 and S4, all exercises.
The extension is missing. Leg and trunk strengthening exercises are necessary.	G: Exercises 1 to 4, 7 to 10, p 13; exercises 1 to 6, p 14 S: S1 and S2, all exercises.
Touch the ground only briefly, plant feet better. Memorize points 1 and 3 on p. 37.	G: — S: S3 and S4, all exercises.
Pull swinging leg forward. Place feet exactly in the direction you are running.	G: — S: S1, exercises 3 and 4.
Whole foot must line up with the toes; then it is impossible to place the feet improperly.	G: — S: S1 and S3, all exercises.

Preparing for Short Distance Running

What Does a Sprinter Need?

As we indicated earlier in the book, the most important factor in sprinting is speed! What is necessary for speed? First, it depends on musculature, since the muscle can only contract if it is strong. Second, it depends on the stride sequence, which is determined especially by the nerve's ability to react quickly. The brain sends messages to the muscles by way of the nerves to tell them whether to contract or relax. The faster each impulse reaches its destination, the faster one stride can follow another.

The difficulty is that, no matter the speed, only the exact muscle needed must receive the message. If the leg must extend, then only the extensor works, while the flexor remains fully relaxed. After extension, it is the exact opposite: the flexor works and the extensor relaxes. If this exchange ceases to work at any point, through incorrect or inexact nerve impulses, tension remains in the other muscle and movement will be hindered and become slower. The nerves, therefore, play an important role; and they can be trained, especially in growing bodies.

Sprinters also need good reaction speed for the start. That is also a property of the nerves.

Finally, sprinters must have endurance, since they become tired and slower after 30 to 40 m during a fast run.

How to Train

In our training program, we need exercises for strength, reaction ability, speed, and for learning the crouch-start technique. The following exercises should be included:

Strength: leg strengthening exercises and acceleration.

Reaction speed: acceleration and short bursts of speed.

Crouch-start: acceleration and the crouch-start itself.

Reaction speed can also be improved through goalkeeping practice and badminton.

It is important for all runners that the track which is used for strength development be at least 20 to 25 m long, but not longer than 50 m.

Break 2 to 4 minutes between the runs.

Where to Train

The track for speed runs must be selected carefully. It can be a part of your endurance route and must be straight for at least 60 m. Uneven ground should be avoided, since it is easy to stumble at greater speeds. You must have a clear view of the area, especially crossing, so that you do not crash full speed into pedestrians or cyclists. If you cannot go to a track and parks, little-used side-walks are suitable. The terrain can also be slightly uphill.

Now test your level of performance so that you can set your next goal. Check your performance against the table norms.

Table 1 Running performance norms for youth.

	Performance (in sec.)					
	Poor Girls Boys (under)		Intermediate Girls Boys (around)		Good Girls Boys (over)	
Youth B (60m)	12.6 11.8 12.1 11.7		11.7 11.0 11.3 10.9		9.5 9.0	
Youth A (60m)	11.8 11.5 11.6 11.3		11.0 10.7 10.8 10.5		9.0 8.5	

S1 Specific Leg Strengthening Exercises — Bounding

Bounding is especially effective because the movements are so similar to those of running. But every stride should be a powerful jump. Pay attention to the following technical points.

1. Each jump should aim for length rather than height, permitting a fast forward movement.

2. The extension of the take-off leg should be energetic.

3. It is assisted powerfully by the swinging leg, the thigh of which should reach the horizontal and remain there until shortly before landing.

4. The upper body is almost upright. There is no bending at the hips.

5. Arms and shoulders swing rhythmically and firmly.

Bounding is generally done over a distance of 20 to 30 m. Depending on the task, different goals can be achieved. Rapid completion of the route demands more speed; longer jumps develop jumping ability.

1. **Bounding over balls or other small obstacles.**
   10 to 12 times = 1 set
   At first the distance between the ball should be no greater than 1 m. Then they can be moved farther and farther apart. How far is the greatest distance you can jump?

2. **Bounding on stairs.**
   8 to 10 times = 1 set
   Take several steps with one jump. Try to reach the top quickly. Also jump up the stairs in the gym.

3. **Bounding from line to line.**
   8 to 10 times = 1 set
   Your feet should land exactly on the marks. Make several rows of marks at varying distances.

4. **Bounding into rings.**
   8 to 10 times = 1 set
   Jump into gymnastic rings or old bicycle tires.

5. **Bounding a set route.**
   6 to 8 times = 1 set
   Bound from house to house, from tree to tree, the length of the penalty area of the soccer field, etc.

The two green figures on every exercise page show flexibility and relaxation exercises that should be performed during the breaks:
a. back arm circles;
b. forward trunk bends.
Practise both several times.

43

1

S2 Specific Leg Strengthening Exercises – Pushing and Pulling

These are primarily fun, partner-exercises. The direct competition between the partners serves its purpose only if they are of approximately equal strength.

The use of great strength is more effective in developing the strength of the extensors, which is crucial for the first steps of a crouch-start. To strengthen the muscles most needed for the start, it is important to push or pull in a strong forward lean, approximately the position used in the start.

In practising these exercises, pay attention to the following.

1. The hips should not bend too much. Instead, push the pelvis forward with each stride.

2. When possible, lift the knee of the swinging leg strongly.

3. If the arms are free, they should assist the leg movement by swinging in the same rhythm.

4. Where only one partner pushes or pulls, the other should only offer just enough resistance that a forward movement is still possible.

44

1. **Truck push.**
   4 to 6 times, 20 m
   The front partner lets himself be pushed, while offering resistance. After every round, the partners change positions.

2. **Pull competition.**
   2 to 3 times
   Each tries to pull the other over a goal line, 4 to 5 m away. Tie the ropes together well so that you do not fall.

3. **Push competition.**
   2 to 3 times
   This task is similar to the pull competition. Arms should always be extended. Do not move sideways.

4. **The horse game.**
   4 to 5 times, 20 m
   The "coachman" is slowly pulled.

5. **Running on the spot, pushing against a wall or tree.**
   5 to 10 seconds.
   In this exercise, try to increase the pressure against the wall while your feet run on the spot. How many double strides can you do in 5 seconds? 10 seconds? A double-stride count: and one—and two— and three.

Flexibility Exercises:
a. Bicycle from a neckstand.
b. Lie on your back; raise legs over head, keeping them straight, and touch toes to the ground behind head.

Speed work

S3 Speed Exercises — Short Bursts of Speed

Speed should gradually increase from an easy jog to a fast sprint. The value of this method is that the greatest part of the route will not be run at full speed. This helps prevent muscles from stiffening up.

Pay Attention to the Following:

1. Begin with runs over 30 to 50 m and increase them gradually to 80 to 120 m.

2. Increase the speed initially through longer strides, and only after through faster strides.

3. During the period of greatest exertion, try to remain as relaxed as when you are jogging.

4. Keep your face relaxed. Smile! Under no circumstances clench your teeth.

5. Run at maximum speed 20 to 25 m, then using minimal strength. Maintain the speed reached, and then coast to a stop.

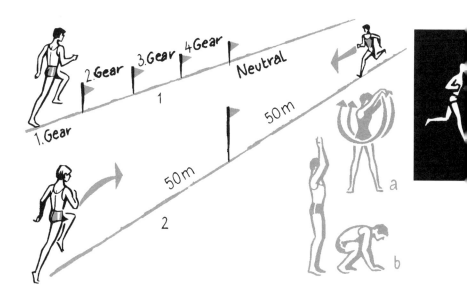

1. **Speed running.**
   3 to 6 times, depending on length
   Every 10 to 20 m put up a flag as
   a check mark. At each flag move
   into the next "gear." The pace is
   increased in the stretch between
   the flags.

2. **Short bursts of speed with
   partners meeting in the middle.**
   5 to 7 times
   In the middle of a 100 m stretch
   is a clearly visible flag. Each
   person starts off at the same
   time from either end and tries to
   meet exactly in the middle at full
   speed. This can also be done
   with two groups of runners.

3. **Short bursts of speed uphill.**
   3 to 5 times
   Very strenuous, it develops
   strength.

4. **Short bursts of speed around
   a curve.**
   4 to 6 times

> **Flexibility Exercises:**
> a. Make backward and forward
>   circles with your arms.
> b. Breathing practice. Stretch
>   yourself up tall and breathe
>   in, crouch down in a ball and
>   breathe out.

S4 Speed Exercises — Acceleration

By acceleration, we mean a sudden and energetic speeding up of the body from a resting position or a slower run. All accelerations, therefore, are actually forms of starts, and for this reason are perfectly suited to preparing you for the crouch-start.

In our picture, you can recognize the two basic forms of acceleration. The girl on the left is demonstrating a falling start. The sudden acceleration can only be achieved when the body falls far forward. It also looks like this from a trot. The feet pound the ground. The body straightens up, only gradually as from the crouch-start. After approximately 20 m, you come out of high gear and let yourself coast for a while in neutral. For this reason, the running track is usually 40 to 60 m long, although you only sprint 20 m.

The boy on the right illustrates the standing start. Here the trunk immediately bends forward in the starting position. Begin first with acceleration from motion: it's easier. For the crouch-start, however, acceleration from a resting position is better. Practise this often.

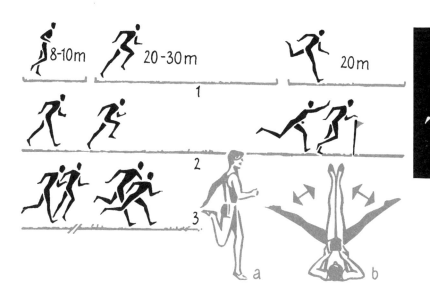

1. Acceleration from a trot.
10 to 12 times

Runners accelerate at a determined spot (street light, corner of house, bush, tree, mark, etc). Later one runner can give the command to accelerate for all.

2. Tag.
10 to 12 times

For this you must form pairs. One partner trots, or stands 2 m in front of the other. At a whistle or a mark, 20 m from the finish line, the pairs accelerate. The first runner must be caught.

3. Races in pairs.
10 to 12 times

Sprint to the finish line from a trotting start, a standing start, or a falling start. Try to beat your partner. Practising acceleration from a squatting position, knee support, and forward support lean help improve the crouch-start. Acceleration from lying prone on the stomach or back is also possible. Also run from a crouch-start.

Flexibility Exercises:
a. trotting with heels high;
b. opening and closing legs from a neckstand.

Winter Competitions

There are several enjoyable games and competitions that can be used where there is enough snow.

1. Sleigh-pushing competition.

The exercise requires at least two people. Push your partner 20 to 30 m on a sleigh. If there are only two of you, the partner being pushed must keep track of the other's time. Then change positions and see who pushes faster. If there is a group, form teams that compete against each other at the same time. The competition will be more difficult if two people are sitting on the sleigh. The partner on the sleigh does not always have to sit; he or she can kneel or lie down.

If the route is on a slight slope, go around a turning point so that the sleigh turns downhill.

2. Long-distance sleigh pushing

A level surface for this competition is essential. The sled and occupant are pushed approximately 15m to a line. The person behind may not cross this line but gives the sleigh a push as hard as possible. Keep track of the distance. The next person tries to do better. Make sure to use a sleigh with the same weight.

The Long Jump

The Long Jump — an Art?

A world-record holder and Olympic champion in the long jump has said:

"Even if the long jump is a traditional track-and-field event, this does not mean that its technique is easy. Anyone who underestimates the difficulty of the long jump usually will not learn all the important points of the movement sequence. With time and practice, it is not at all difficult to learn the basics.

Distance is achieved through high speed during the run-up, and an explosive take-off. The faster the run-up becomes as performance improves, the less time is available to complete the take-off (for the world's best, only one tenth of a second). The effective combination of run-up and take-off is the "art" in long-jumping. What makes it difficult is that the board must also be hit as accurately as possible. As a student, I had problems with this. But in the two-year period before the Olympic games that I was jumping in competitions only two of my attempts were declared invalid. I was able to become a "millimetre jumper" only after determined training. So, you should practise the run-off/take-off combination conscientiously, and always aim for accuracy on the board."

The Stride Long Jump

There are several different techniques in long jumping, and the question immediately arises which is best. To understand the answer, you must realize that jumping techniques actually differ only in flight movements, which overall have the least influence on the distance of the jump. They serve to balance your weight and prepare you for landing. It is not possible to land in a squatting position; so, the body must be extended in flight. For this reason the world's best jumpers prefer the hitch-kick technique, in which the jumper "runs" in the air. Some 8 m jumpers actually make 3 1/2 strides in flight before they land. Naturally that number is only possible when you jump close to 8 m. With smaller distances, 2 1/2 strides are taken. Jumps of at least 4.5 to 5.0 m are needed for this number. Initially you can make only one stride in the air and then land. That is not really running in the air. So we call this form the "stride-long jump." It is easy to do and it is preferable to the float style.

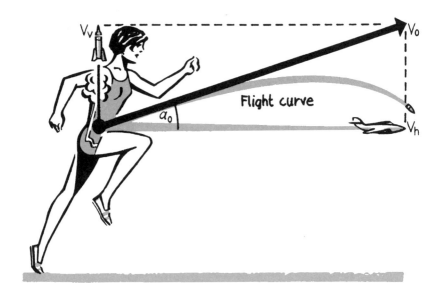

Technique of the Stride-Long Jump

How long the body remains in flight depends on the speed of the jumper at take-off: the greater the take-off speed, the longer the jumper can remain in the air. How far or how high the jump is depends on the angle of take-off: a small angle means a farther jump, a larger angle, a higher jump.

The partial speeds (V_o) determine this angle: the horizontal speed (V_h) plus the vertical speed (V_v). (See illustration.) The flight will be steeper or flatter depending on which of the two speeds is greater. In long jumping, V_h must be approximately three times greater than V_v. The speed V_h is mainly the result of the run-up. The faster it is, the greater V_h will be. V_v can only originate in the take-off.

From these basic laws you can see that the run-up and take-off are the most important factors of long jumping. Speed and take-off power, on the one hand, and the technique of the take-off, on the other, are the foundations for your performance.

Important Points for the Run-Up

● For children, the run-up should be 12 to 16 running strides. Measure the area accordingly.

● Always begin the run-up with the same foot. The first stride of the run-up must always be the same length so that you take-off from the board. Use check marks to get it right (see illustration).

● Try to achieve a high speed quickly. You must be at your fastest speed at the moment you reach the board. Do you remember why? If not read page 54 once more.

● Shortly before the take-off, the upper body straightens to get into the proper take-off position.

● During the run-up, you must remain totally relaxed. At the start, concentrate on speed not the take-off.

● The biggest mistake at take-off is lengthening or shortening the strides just before the board in order to take-off in exactly the right place. One way or the other, the result is that you are too slow to achieve a good jump.

It is not enough to achieve the extension of the take-off leg shown here, you have to finish at the right time as well.

M1

The most serious and the most common mistake at take-off is the failure to extend the swinging leg quickly enough. You waste the high speed achieved in the run-up. The mistake can't be illustrated on paper. It must be observed during the jump. The extension illustrated above must be completed. Keep this firmly in mind.

M2

Paul extends well, but:
His head ....
His back ....
Exaggeration of the extension puts the body's center of gravity in a poor relation to the take-off leg. He may lose his balance.

Important Points for the Take-Off

● The take-off stride is significantly faster than all the running steps that came before. The next foot is planted on the board extremely explosively. Concentrate on this!

● The heels only touch the ground briefly. The foot rolls quickly on the ball. You must feel that you are gripping the board with your foot and kicking it backwards.

● The energetic extension of the hip and knee joints that comes after should involve the whole body.

● At the same time, bring the swinging leg up until the thigh is horizontal and knee is sharply bent.

● The upper body is upright; the eyes straight ahead.

● Arms assist the take-off through their alternating swings (lift shoulders sharply).

M3

Elizabeth wants to achieve a high flight path, but:
Her trunk ....
Her take-off leg ....
These problems may hinder the run-up speed so much that the height of the jump cannot compensate.

M4

What can Tom do to improve?
His swinging leg ....
His upper body ....
Not only will he make too flat a jump, he will fail to bring his legs far enough forward in landing. How can he improve his jump?

M5

How is Tom jumping here?
His upper body ....
His swinging leg ....
This position in flight is usually the result of a mistake in the take-off. Look for the cause on page 57. Only when he corrects this mistake will Tom be able to jump farther.

M6

John is about to land. At this stage:
His legs must ....
His upper body must ....
He is no longer able to control the landing. He will end the flight too soon and lose 30 to 40 cm.

Important Points for the Flight Phase

- The take-off position is held during the first part of the flight. Tell yourself: "F-L-Y!"

- The upper body remains at least upright, even better is a slight backward lean.

- After the exertion of the take-off the take-off leg remains totally relaxed behind the body.

- Just before landing, swing the legs and the upper body forward like a jack-knife. Now tell yourself: "Ahead!"

- Both legs are at the same height, almost horizontal over the landing pit. The upper body rests on the knees.

- The arms fall far back and down. The flight path is used advantageously in this body position.

M7

Why is Christine twisting like that? She leaned a bit too far left at take-off and, as a result, lost her balance during flight. She will now have difficulty landing properly. What must she do?

M8

What jump is that?
It is a .... jump.
His legs and trunk ....
With this body position you can easily lose your balance. Often the take-off will also suffer, since the hips are not extended.

M9

What is Ted doing wrong?
His feet ....
As a result, he unnecessarily loses many centimetres in the length covered. Show him how he can avoid this. Look at the mistake table.

M10

That does not work well!
His knee joints ....
His feet land far forward, but in this position he can't bring his body over the landing spot and will fall backward.

Things to watch for when landing:

- The legs are forward, almost extended but not stiff.
- The knees bend as soon as the heels touch the ground.
- The upper body straightens somewhat, so that the hips can be pushed forward and the body weight moved over the supporting area.
- At this point, the buttocks must be prevented from touching the ground too soon.

- The feet land parallel to each other. The landing spot is correct if you can just throw yourself forward or sideways beside your feet.
- The arms are at first behind the body and encourage the body's motion by swinging forward.
- Leave the landing pit by the front.

M11

This is a common mistake.
His hands ....
Sometimes it is also the buttocks.
Either the same mistake has been made as in picture 10 or the legs are too far forward. In both cases, you have to support yourself from behind.

M12

This student dives forward out of the landing pit and still has a lot of momentum. The mistake is:
His feet ....
What other mistakes can cause this?
Write them down: ....

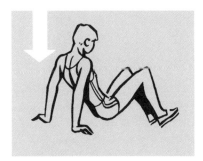

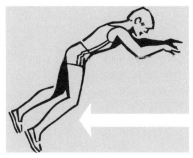

Illustrated Summary Table of Mistakes

Mistake	Illustration
Mistake	**Illustration**
M2 Head held improperly — hollow back posture.	
M3 Body leans too far backward, the take-off leg pushes down.	
M4 Upper body leans too far forward, poor use of swinging leg.	
M5 Upper body is too far forward, swinging leg is not in the stride position.	
M6 Legs are not high enough for the landing.	
M7 Off-balance position in flight forces correcting movements.	
M8 Squat in flight - outdated technique of the float style.	
M9 Feet are not parallel in landing.	
M10 Knees too stiff on landing.	
M11 Supports weight with hands.	
M12 Feet land too soon, leading to motion out of the landing pit.	

Correction of Mistakes and Choice of Exercises

Correction	Exercise
Hold head level and look past the landing pit.	G: 4, p. 13. S: L2, all exercises.
Extend yourself before take-off. Set feet down quickly.	G: 10, p. 13. S: L1, exercise 1 and 3; L3, all exercises.
Before take-off straighten out of forward lean.	G: — S: L4, exercise 2.
Hold the take-off position.	G: — S: L2 and L3, all exercises.
Straighten up more at take-off —strengthen stomach muscles.	G: 7 to 12, p. 13. S: L3, all exercises.
Keep the take-off stride in a straight line.	G: 1 to 3, p. 14. S: L4, all exercises.
Extend yourself at take-off and hold this position.	G: 1, 3, and 4, p. 13. S: L2 and L3, all exercises.
Bring feet parallel in flight.	G: 2 and 9, p. 13. S: Competition forms, p.72.
Relax knees and hips upon touching the ground.	G: 4, 6, and 9, p. 14. S: —
When there is danger of falling backward, shove hips forward	G: 3 and 4, p.14. S: All relaxion exercises, L1 to L4.
Straighten up more at take-off—stomach muscle exercises.	G: 7 to 12, p. 14. S: L2 and L3, all exercises.

Preparing for the Long Jump

Where to Jump

Almost all the exercises that we have chosen for specific long jump preparation can be done without a landing pit. What is important is a firm, level take-off surface. Grass surfaces are particularly suitable; when the grass is wet, an incorrect jump will only lead to sliding. If you can make the ground softer for landing, you should do so. Sand will provide for a safe landing. Deep water is also good for long jump practice. You must be careful that the take-off point is not slippery. Avoid injury! Jump only where you will not disturb or be disturbed by other people.

How to Measure Jumps

In long jumping, the distance is always measured from the last print or impression of the heels on landing to the front edge of the take-off board. The distance is always measured at the board, and never at the landing spot in the pit. Throwing events are exactly the same. If you don't have a tape measure, do this :

a. Determine the length of your foot and measure the distance of the jump with your feet. Multiply the number of footsteps by the length of your feet to arrive at the approximate distance.

b. Mark every 10 cm on a string with a pen, using a ruler. Make a knot every meter.

How to Train

The important points have already been listed on page 54. Three of these are crucial and must be mastered.

Speed is acquired through sprint training. In addition to speed, the long jumper must take-off from the board as accurately as possible. If you jump too soon, you lose distance, since the distance is measured from the board. If you over-step the board, the jump is invalid. You cannot begin practising run-up accuracy too soon! So you should combine sprinting practice with run-ups by accelerating over 20 m to a mark that you must hit with your take-off leg.

Do not look down when running: you can check whether you have hit the board after the jump. You can recognize your foot print better if you rake the ground lightly around the mark so that the sole of the foot makes a clearer impression.

Push-off strength is developed through general leg-strengthening and jumping exercises in the following pages.

Special jumping exercises teach the proper take-off technique. Pay attention to the following.

1. Practise short sets, in the precise number we have given for each exercise.

2. Practise only as long as you are able to take-off explosively.

3. Combine all special exercises with fast run-ups.

4. Try to reach the greatest distance with every jump.

The table gives you information about your level of performance. Can you find a relationship between it and your ability to sprint?

Table 2 Jumping performance norms for youth.

	Performance (in m)					
	Poor Girls Boys (under)		Intermediate Girls Boys (around)		Good Girls Boys (over)	
Youth B	1.90 2.10	2.20 2.40	2.40 2.60	2.70 2.90	3.40	3.80
Youth A	2.20 2.45	2.50 2.70	2.80 3.00	3.00 3.30	4.20	4.80

L1 Jumping from a Rapid Run-Up

You should land and bounce back up like a rubber ball that rebounds after impact. Only with skillful take-offs is this achieved. You must make a "rubber-ball landing."

The illustration above shows how the foot should land:

1. The swinging leg is sharply bent in flight.

2. Shortly before landing, the lower leg swings forward, in order to grip the ground as far forward as possible. The knee remains slightly bent.

3. From this point on, the whole leg lowers from the hip, moving down and back.

4. As a result, the leg is moving in the direction of motion rather than against it on landing. The foot should now quickly roll onto the sole, since the heels cannot take the whole weight of the body.

5. The process resembles a "gripping" or "pawing" movement. Your feet move in a similar way when you run on a rolling cylinder.

1. **Multiple jumps from a five-stride run-up.**
6 to 8 times
Mark the run-up so that the last jump ends in the landing pit, sand hill, or sandbox.

2. **Jumping on boxes.**
6 to 8 times
Use either a set of stairs or build a set of "box stairs" in the gymnasium. Jump from a short run-up. (Leave the greatest possible space between the boxes.)

3. **Jump between bars.**
4 to 6 times
Lay bars on the ground in parallel lines 1.8 m to 2 m apart. Jump through them first in a straight line, and then more and more on an angle. You may touch the ground only once between two lines. Try jumping diagonally from one corner to the other.

4. **Jumping over low obstacles.**
6 to 8 times
As obstacles, use stretched, elevated elastic bands or place balls, wooden blocks, or similar objects in a row at the appropriate points. Increase the distance.

Flexibility exercises
a. Bend trunk backwards (hands grab heels);
b. From a hurdle position, bend trunk forwards.

L2 Jumping over Wide Obstacles

Here are some simpler forms of long jumping that you can practise almost any time: jumping over puddles, small streams, ditches, and so on. The important thing is to get over the obstacle with an energetic jump. Afterwards you must be able to run on without pausing. If you succeed at this, you can try jumping over several such obstacles, one after another. The obstacles should be low but as wide as possible, so that you are forced to jump quickly and power-fully.

Pay attention to the following details:

1. There must be a fast run-up before each series of jumps.

2. Put the swinging leg down quickly as possible.

3. Pull the swinging leg energeti-cally horizontal. The upper body is upright. Extend yourself in flight.

4. On landing, set the swinging leg down springily so that you can continue running immediately.

1. **Jumping from mat to mat.**
   6 to 8 times
   From a fast run-up, jump over the space between each mat. The distance between the mats should be such that only one extra stride on the mats is necessary.

2. **Jumping on boxes.**
   6 to 8 times
   As in the first exercise. Be careful when increasing the distances: do not land to close to the edge of the box. You could slip and sprain or break your ankle.

3. **From "island to island."**
   6 to 8 times
   This is simpler form of the first two exercises. Draw "islands" on the ground, and make several rows of them at various distances apart. Practise jumping in the row where you are just able to jump over the "water."

4. **Zone jumping.**
   12 to 15 times
   Draw two lines to make a wide area that increases on one side. Jump over the widest zone you can.

Flexibility exercises
a. Kneel and bend trunk backwards (touch head to floor).
b. Stand in a straddle position and bend trunk sideways.

L3 Jumping over Double Obstacles

1. **Jump over low elastic bands.**
   6 to 8 times
   Stretch the bands at a height of 25 to 30 cm at most, but place them at least 1.8 to 2 m apart. Set up several such obstacles in a row, one after the other. You should leave room for 3 to 5 strides between each obstacle. Try to recover your speed with the strides between each obstacle. The obstacles should be wide enough that you can just barely jump over them.

2. **Jumping over rows of pins.**
   6 to 8 times
   Distances and execution as in the first exercise.

3. **Jumping over boxes.**
   6 to 8 times
   This time you do not jump onto the boxes, but over them. Run quickly between the obstacles. Good jumpers should raise the height of the boxes.

Flexibility Exercises:
a. Standing in a straddle position, bend trunk sideways.
b. Sitting in a hurdle position, bend trunk backwards.

70

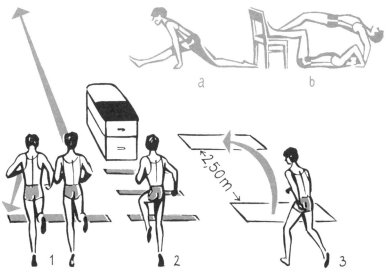

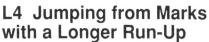

L4 Jumping from Marks with a Longer Run-Up

1. The two boys jump very differently; the jumper on the right is looking straight ahead — that is correct! The one on the left is making the crucial mistake of watching whether his foot hits the take-off mark.

2. **Jumping onto a box at half-height.**
   8 to 10 times
   Begin by jumping from a line approximately 1 m away. Then move the take-off point further and further from the box. Always try to jump onto the middle of the box. Draw a chalk line there.

3. **Jumping from one mark to another.**
   10 to 15 times

The take-off mark should be 40 to 50 cm wide, and the finish line somewhat narrower. The space between should be so great that you are barely able to jump over it from a fast run-up. Increase the distance in the next training session.

71

1

2

Here are two practice competitions:

1. Jumping with a partner.
One competitor from each of two teams jumps. The two jumpers start off at the same time and take-off next to each other from the board. Whoever jumps the farthest gets a point for his or her team.

2. Point-jumping.
Pick out the minimum distance for each point in the performance table on page 136 and mark each with an elastic band. This is how you make the point zones. Who can achieve the best average after 6 to 8 jumps?

The High Jump

The Take-Off — the Decisive Factor

A world-record holder and Olympic champion in the high jump has said:

"Coaches and jumpers have taught us that the secret of high jumping is in the take-off. Training for the take-off must begin early; it is very difficult to acquire it later.

When training alone, practise as many jumps as possible with steep light curves using run-ups of different lengths and speeds. Practise jumping from the right and the left. The technique of clearing the bar is secondary. Your improvised jumping facilities usually aren't right to practise clearing the bar properly. The mistakes in take-off and flight that result are very difficult to eliminate later on."

Technique of the High Jump

Float style, scissors, eastern cut-off, western roll, straddle jump and the flop — are all of these totally different jumps? No. Actually it is better to speak of different methods of clearing the bar. The run-up and take-off are basically the same in all of them.

Run-up and take-off have the greatest influence on the height of the jump. Anyone who cannot take-off properly will not achieve height, even using the most sophisticated flight movements.

Nevertheless, we must give the modern bar-clearing methods their due. Look at the illustration. All jumpers will reach the same height at their bodies' centers of gravity. But because of the different positions over the bar, the distance of the lowest body part to the center of gravity is different. That is why the float-style jumper reaches the lowest height, while the others take better advantage of their flight height. Best of all, are the straddle and the flop jumpers.

You should learn all these variations. But watch out: beginners are easily tempted to dive in the straddle jump, instead of taking off upward. By doing this, they decrease height considerably, and the loss cannot be made up.

Remember the proper take-off.

Pay attention to our training hints on page 79.

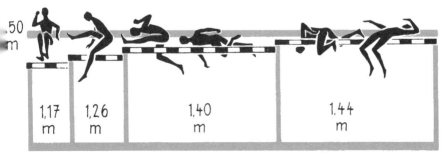

.50 m

1,17 m   1,26 m   1,40 m   1,44 m

Establishing the Run-Up

The run-up is measured from the take-off position to the starting point of the run-up. The take-off position is opposite the end of the first quarter of the bar, and approximately 50 to 70 cm away from it. Measure how many of your foot lengths this is. Mark the take-off point (P2) and draw a line from here to the mid point of the bar (P1). The extension of this line is the proper run-up angle. If you find that another angle works better for you, just move P2 to the left or right. Measure that also, so that you can find your angle quickly with any high jump stand.

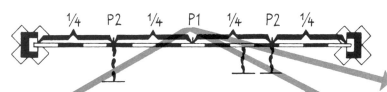

¼   P2   ¼   P1   ¼   P2   ¼

Take-off position
for left foot jumper

Take-off position
for right foot jumper

Important Points for the Straddle Jump:

- The run-up for the straddle jump follows a straight line at an 25° to 45° angle to the bar from the side of the take-off leg.

- Five to seven strides in the run-up are enough.

- The run-up pace is moderate.

- Accelerate only on the first 3 to 5 strides. Concentrate on the take-off on the last two strides.

- The second last stride is flat and long. It leads to a bent position of the swinging leg. Both arms are behind the body.

- As the take-off leg is rapidly planted over the heels, push the hips forward energetically. The body then achieves the proper thrust position. The chin must be against the chest.

M1

What mistake do you recognize here? The runway is not ....

....

The run-up angle is no longer correct. As a result, you dive over the bar. Find a way to correct this mistake.

M2

Andrew does concentrate on the take-off, but:
His next-to-last stride ....

....

As a result the transition to the last stride lacks fluidity, and the take-off is too slow.

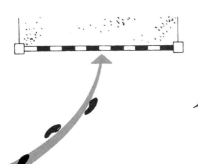

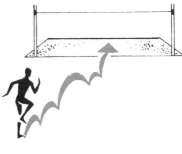

M3

You must avoid this mistake.
The upper body ....
The swinging leg ....
This jump will become a dive that not only makes a low body position possible, but also leads to a flat flight curve.

M4

The swinging leg is extended, but:
His hips ....
As a result, the strength of the take-off leg does not affect the body totally. In addition, the muscles of the buttocks are not working along with the others. Which exercises would you use to correct this mistake?

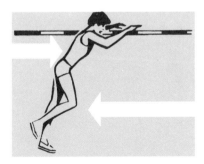

Important Points for the Take-Off for the Straddle Jump

- The take-off leg begins an energetic extension immediately after the foot has been planted.

- The hips do not give out under the strong pressure, but must be pushed actively forward and up.

- The upper body remains above the take-off leg, and does not bend toward the bar. At the same time it leans slightly, as if the jumper were tightly coiled like a spring before take-off.

- The swinging leg supports the take-off considerably if it is extended and swung as high as possible over the bar by means of a rapid forward swing of the lower leg.

- Both arms are swung forward and up at the same time as the swinging leg.

- Just before take-off, the jumper turns toward the bar.

M5

The extension is explosive, but:
Her upper body ....
Her head ....
Here also, the strength of the take-off is lost because the jumper reaches for the bar too soon.

M6

What is wrong here, despite good extension? ....
....
With this jump, valuable strength for the momentum is lost. Also, the body's centre of gravity is too low when the athlete leaves the ground.

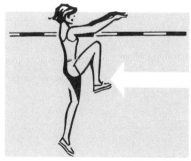

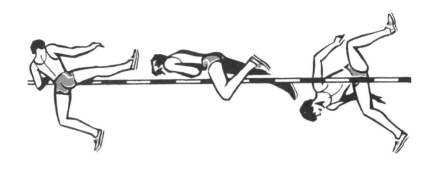

M7

Angela is straddling the bar well, but:
Her head ....
Explain to her that, as a result, her back hollows and her pelvis is pushed down. As a result, she will knock the bar down. How should she hold her head?

M8

Leonard is already thinking about the landing, but:
His head and upper body ....
....
Because of this, a twisting occurs that, at this stage of the straddle, hinders the take-off leg. He will knock the bar down.

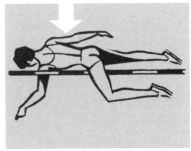

Important Points for Clearing the Bar

- The body is turned towards the bar during the entire flight phase. The body rotates around the bar as momentum carries the jumper over the bar.

- The body is extended once over the bar, and almost parallel to it. The take-off leg is drawn up and the arms are held close to the body.

- The upper body and the swinging leg drop rapidly down on the other side of the bar.

- The knee of the take-off leg straddles outward at the same time to avoid the bar. The toes of the take-off leg must be turned. That is the most important movement.

- The chin should always press against the chest to prevent a hollow back position.

- The swinging leg and the hand on that side land first. The impact is absorbed by rolling onto the hips.

M9

This is a typical beginner's mistake. Can you recognize it?
His take-off leg ....
The knee and toes of his take-off leg
....
As a result, it is harder for the hips to avoid the bar because the rotation is slowed down.

M10

The rotation is right, but:
Her body ....
If the jumper's center of gravity is too high, the main advantage of the straddle jump—a low clearance height—is lost.

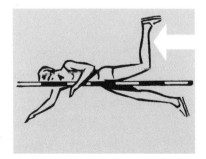

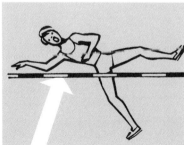

Illustrated Summary Table of Mistakes

Mistake	Illustration
Mistake	**Illustration**
M3 Upper body bends forward — the swinging leg is not planted, the jumper "dives."	
M4 The hips give out backwards as the leg is swinging.	
M5 Too far from the bar.	
M6 The swinging leg is bent.	
M7 Head raised — hollow back position.	
M8 Upper body rotated improperly — face and chest are toward the bar.	
M9 The take-off leg is kicked back and up — it does not straddle outward.	
M10 The body is not parallel to the bar — it is still too upright.	

Correction of Mistakes and Choice of Exercises

Correction	Exercise
Plant the swinging leg firmly and hold the body straight at take-off.	G: 8, p.13. S: H1 and H2, all exercises; H4, exercise 1 and 2.
At take-off, straighten up and push hips firmly forward.	G: 3, 4, 5, 11, 12, p.14. S: H1 and H2, all exercises.
Practise the vertical jump by making many jumps without rotation.	G: 1 to 3, p.13. S: H1 and H2, all exercises.
Jumps and exercises swinging the extended leg — stomach exercises.	G: 10, 11, and 12, p.14. S: H2, exercise 1; H4, all exercises.
When jumping always press chin to chest. During the straddle jump, press head to the bar.	G: — S: H3, all exercises with rotation.
In flight always look at the bar! Practise several jumps with rotation.	G: — S: H3, do all exercises with rotation.
Practise straddling in a standing position and with simple jumps.	G: Relaxation exercise (a), p.11. S: H2 and H3, all exercises as rotation jumps with straddling.
Straddle jump over higher bars.	G: — S: Straddle jump with a check mark for the hand on swinging leg side.

The Fosbury Flop

The run-up starts on the side of the swinging leg. It should be run fast and on a curve. The curve is greatest for the last three strides. Its radius is 6 m for a 3-stride run-up, 7 m for a 5-stride run-up, and 8 m for a 7-stride run-up.

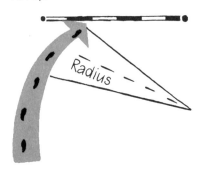

The Take-off

● Take-off with the leg furthest from the bar.

● The extension follows quickly, as vertically as possible. At first there is no rotation of the back toward the bar.

● The leg swings energetically up toward the inside. The knee joint is bent. The swinging direction varies 15° to 20° from the running direction. In this way the back begins to rotate toward the bar.

● The eyes are on the pole; the head looks over the shoulder on the swinging leg side, away from the direction of rotation.

Clearing the Bar

● After the take-off, the swinging leg falls to join the relaxed take-off leg. The body is long and rotates quickly into the necessary position with the back to the bar. The body twists upward.

● As soon as the shoulders have cleared the bar, the hips are pushed forward. The body forms a "bridge" over the bar (hollow back).

● After the buttocks have also cleared the bar, the hips are quickly bent and the knees straightened. Now the body forms an "L." (Picture 6)

The Landing

● The outspread arms land first. Then the jumper falls on his back. The "L-position" should be maintained during this phase of the jump. The muscles should be tensed so that the trunk cannot be sprained.

● This landing is only safe on special surfaces. Only practise where the proper landing surface is available and where you can be supervised by a trainer or teacher. Do not—under any circumstances—jump onto a sand pile.

Preparing for the High Jump

Where to Jump

On first consideration, this problem is hard to solve, since with modern jumping techniques you fall on your back. Therefore a very soft landing surface is definitely necessary. We have considered that in our choice of exercises: only a few require a soft landing surface.

Two conditions are necessary: a level and firm take-off area and an obstacle to jump over. Firm take-off areas can be found on paths or squares that are gravelled or firmly trampled. Grass offers reasonable safety in dry weather only. Even then spikes are necessary.

An obstacle is easier to find. An elastic 3 to 4 m long is very good. You can tie this to anything; fence posts, pickets, bushes, and the like. Best of all are especially made support poles that must be driven into the ground. Mark heights on the poles, being careful to drive them into the ground precisely to the zero mark. The straddle jump and the flop should never be practised without a proper landing area. Again, these jumps are only possible with a special equipment.

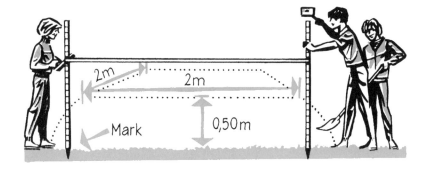

2m 2m Mark 0,50m

How to Train

Under no circumstances begin practising the straddle jump without acquiring the necessary take-off strength and jumping skill. The exercises on the next pages are designed for this purpose.

With all jumps, try to jump high, not far. Only short run-ups are necessary. The proper push-off position, hips forward and the leg swinging quickly, is especially important.

Always make sure that your landing is close to the take-off point. All jumps with rotation are direct preparation exercises for the straddle jump and the flop. Practise them often in your training program.

Under no circumstances combine high jump and long jump exercises in one training session. The change-over is difficult and is not helpful for either types of jump. But general leg-strengthening exercises on page 13 are good for all jumping, including high jumping.

Don't forget flexibility exercises. An inflexible high jumper won't make the championships!

Properly prepared, you may attempt the straddle jump. To start, don't practise alone. Practise with two or three friends, so that you can point out each other's mistakes. You may also practise before your coach or teacher.

The following table will help you estimate your performance level. Your goal should be to reach the next ability level.

Table 3 High-jumping performance norms for youth.

	Performance (in m)					
	Poor Girls Boys (under)		Intermediate Girls Boys (around)		Good Girls Boys (over)	
Youth B	0.55	0.60	0.70	0.80	1.10	1.20
	0.65	0.70	0.80	0.85		
Youth A	0.70	0.75	0.85	0.90	1.30	1.40
	0.75	0.80	0.95	1.00		

H1 Jumping High Objects

Everyone has tried this kind of jumping for fun. Your knowledge of proper take-off techniques will make you better at it.

Again, remember the following technical details:

1. Do not run up too fast. Take only 3 to 7 run-up strides. As preparation for the flop, curved run-ups work well.

2. Before the take-off, go a little deeper, in order to have enough momentum for an energetic and powerful take-off.

3. Plant the almost extended take-off leg quickly so that it works as a lever.

4. At the same time, push the hips forward and upward. In this way you are in the proper position for a steep jump.

5. Take-off a short distance before the target so that you jump steeply and with height.

1. **Zone jumping for an elastic band.**
   10 to 12 times
   Stretch the elastic high enough that it is relatively easy to jump. Draw lines for the run-up zones and try to jump up and touch the elastic in the zone nearest the highest end.

2. **Jumping for branches.**
   10 to 12 times
   Look first for lower and then higher branches.

3. **Hit the ball with your head.**
   10 to 12 times
   Hang a rubber ball in a net or on a string just high enough that you can jump and hit it with your head.

4. **Jumping up large trees.**
   6 to 8 times
   Trees growing on an angle are best. After a short run-up land high with your swinging leg, make another step upward with your take-off leg, and then, after a quick turn, jump down.

Flexibility Exercises:
a. Standing with one leg stretched out in front on a box, bend your trunk forward. Hands move with the trunk.
b. Go down on one knee and spring back up.

H2 Jumping over High Obstacles

This is the start of proper high jumping. The more you do, the easier it
will be to clear the bar later on.

Besides improving your take-off
power, these exercises are meant to
develop your jumping skill, especially
the transition from run-up to take-off.
Pay attention to the characteristics
of the take-off. Re-read page 88,
numbers 1 to 5.

For these jumps, concentrate
on using the fast movement of the
swinging leg. The girls in the picture
practise the swing with an extended
leg for the straddle and the eastern
cut-off. Practise this often.

Pay attention to the following:

1. The leg should swing as high
   and as long as possible. The
   toes are pointed.

2. When over the obstacle, the
   swinging leg remains in front of
   you for control, and only the take-
   off leg is tucked under the body.

3. Land on the take-off leg with a
   slight backward lean and immediately run on.

1. **Jumping from a landing zone to a take-off zone.**
   10 to 12 times
   Both zones are 80 to 90 cm in front of or behind the obstacle.

2. **"Window jumping."**
   12 to 15 times
   For this exercise you need 2 jumping lines that are stretched parallel to each other. You should jump over the first and land in front of the second without touching it. Jump as if you were jumping into a horizontal window. Make the window narrower and narrower.

3. **Continuous jumps.**
   4 to 6 times
   Build at least 3 obstacles one after another that you are barely able to clear.
   Make 1 or 2 strides between the obstacles.

4. **"Acrobatic jumping."**
   4 to 6 times
   As in exercise 3, but each obstacle is higher than the one before. The last one can be higher than you can now jump. How long will it be before you can clear this height?

Flexibility Exercises:
a. With one leg stretched out behind and resting on something, bend trunk backward.
b. Standing and leaning forward, rotate trunk with relaxed moving arms.

H3 Jumping with a Longer Flight Phase

The flight phase is lengthened by jumping off a spring board or by having the take-off area higher than the landing area. Jumping from slopes or into water (steep banks of lakes or ponds, old gravel pits) create similar conditions. If these conditions can't be found, use a piece of elastic. You can even practise this kind of jumping without an obstacle. (But it is always better when you are forced by an obstacle to jump high.)

Since you must make certain movements when jumping, in these exercises you will practise getting an overview of the flight and controlling the body. These skills are essential to clearing the bar.

We have chosen only a few examples. Think up your own exercises. For the straddle jump, think up exercises that require rotation.

Make sure that you can land safely!

When you jump from a greater height, the landing surface must be soft!

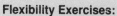

1. **Jumping off the spring board.**
   10 to 12 times
   Jump over the obstacle with legs spread and stretched out in front. Touch your feet with your hands (straddle vault).
2. **Jumping with a landing target.**
   10 to 12 times
   As a target, use a simple ring or even a tire. Also, do rotation jumps into the tire.
3. **Jumping from a raised take-off area.**
   12 to 15 times
   Do not simply jump down. Jump as high as possible. "Window jumping" is also recommended (see p. 89).
4. **Group jumping into target rings.**
   8 to 10 times

A good exercise for a training group. Each jumper must jump into a different ring. The closer to each other you take-off, the more exciting the exercise. Make sure you aim for the right ring.

Flexibility Exercises:
a. From a front push-up position, rotate the hips so that the take-off leg touches the ground with its heel on the far side of the swinging leg (shoulders do not move).
b. Standing in a straddle position with hands on hips, bend trunk sideways.

H4 Exercising the Swinging Leg

The swinging leg has an important function: supporting the take-off leg. But it can only do so when it can swing its entire length above the bar quickly. This, in turn, depends on the strength of the stomach muscles and on the flexibility of the leg from the hip joint.

Our leg exercises should help to develop these characteristics. Look again at the swinging movement on page 78.

The leg swings forward in a bent position, until it passes the take-off leg. At this moment, the leg extends fully with a snapping movement of the lower leg. The toes are pointed. During the swing, the hips do not give out downward. That would work against your take-off extension.

Try this movement first in a standing position. You can always combine it with one of the take-off exercises or with an actual take-off. As soon as you start jumping with a run-up, pay strict attention that you grip is firm at the take-off point. If you slide, the swinging leg will make you fall on your back.

1 2 a b 3 4 How many m?

1. **Competitive leg swinging against a wall.**
   6 to 8 times
   Stand at an angle with the take-off leg closer to the wall. The hand closest is on the wall for support. Now, using a powerful swing of the outer leg, try to touch the wall high up with your toes. Who can kick the highest above their own body height?

2. **Kicking with the swinging leg.**
   6 to 8 times
   The swinging leg kicks a ball suspended high in the air. How high can you kick?

3. **Leg swinging from a horizontal position.**
   12 to 15 times

Lie on your back on a table so that the swinging leg hangs down the side. From there, you swing it powerfully upward. This effect increases when you swing against the resistance of a strong elastic band.

4. **Flinging the medicine ball.**
   6 to 8 times
   A sand bag can also be used (3 to 4 kg).

Flexibility exercises:
a. In a standing position, swing one leg rapidly backwards and forwards.
b. Bicycling from a stretch hang.

95

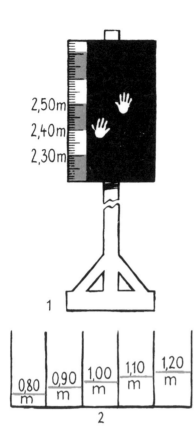

2,50m
2,40m
2,30m

1

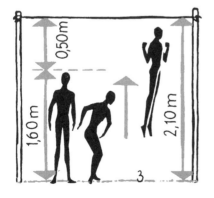

0,80 m | 0,90 m | 1,00 m | 1,10 m | 1,20 m

2

0,50 m
1,60 m
2,10 m
3

A Few Interesting Competitions

1. Jump up the blackboard.

Glue a measuring device to the edge of a blackboard (cardboard, wood, or plastic) high enough so that you can only touch it when you jump. Whiten your hand with chalk. The board will record your height very accurately. The winner is the one who achieves the greatest difference between his or her standing and jumping heights.

2. Team high jumping.

Two or more teams pick a jumper from their team for each height. The player who can jump without touching the marker or band wins a point for the team.

3. Stretch jumping from a standing position.

Jump on two legs from a standing position toward an elastic band stretched tightly above your head. If you can touch the line with your head, move the line higher and find out at what height you can just reach it. The difference between the height of the elastic and your own height is the actual jumping height. This is a good way to test your take-off power.

Rounders, Club and Javelin Throwing

Improve Your Throwing

One world-record holder in javelin throwing describes her development: "As a child I enjoyed throwing very much. It never really occurred to me that throwing should be hard for girls. Even then, I could beat many boys in my class at throwing, probably because I practised more. Although I decided quite early to concentrate on track and field—I did not just throw. Just the opposite. With all-around training, I succeeded in achieving good performance in other events as well. I really enjoyed testing my strength in handball and soccer. The high level of mobility in my shoulder is also due to gymnastics and swimming, because these were a big part of my early training. My advice to girls is: remain active in various sports, especially throwing sports. Good throwing technique, and the capacity to throw long distances takes, above all, practise."

The Technique of the Powerful Throw

Rounders Throw—Club Throw—Javelin Throw

Similarities

1. The three objects are all thrown above the shoulder with a powerful whip-like movement.

2. The run-up is on a 4 m wide runway. During the run-up, the thrower is not allowed to rotate.

3. The transition to the throw is accomplished with the help of an "impulse stride" made with the right leg forward. It is the second-to-last stride in the run-up.

4. The legs support the throw by extending in turn — first the right, then the left.

   The body is checked with a long stride.

Differences

1. The objects are held differently.

2. The run-up in ball-throwing is considerably shorter than in club and javelin throwing.

3. In club and javelin throwing, there is a backward movement of the throwing arm. In ball-throwing, the arm starts at the back.

4. Because of their different flight characteristics, the ball and the club have a ballistic flight curve, while the javelin has an aerodynamic flight curve with a different angle.

5. As a result, the ball and club are in a lower throwing position (between the hips and shoulders) than the javelin (above the shoulder).

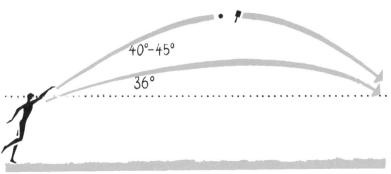

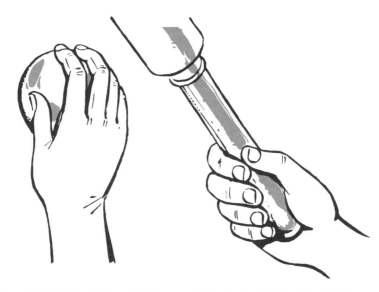

How to Hold the Ball and Club

1. The forefinger and middle finger are behind the ball, the thumb and ring finger push forward against it from either side.

2. The club is held firmly in the hand. Thumb and forefinger grasp it at the thickest part.

3. The hand is relaxed.

Mistakes in Holding the Ball

1. The ball rests cupped in the palm of the hand, all fingers are closed around it.

2. Only the thumb and forefinger hold onto the ball. In both cases, letting go of the ball early enough is hindered. (The ball flies too flat or too steep.)

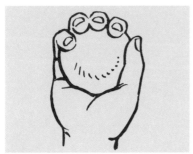

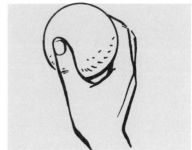

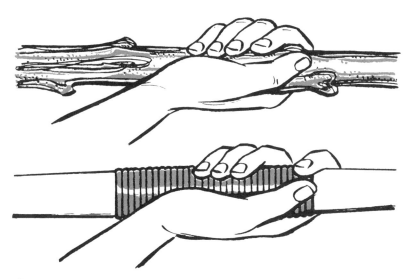

Gripping the Spear and Javelin

1. The shaft lies in the long hollow of the hand.

2. The thumb and forefinger close around it behind the binding (spear—behind the thickest part of the branch).

3. The palm of the hand is up and the hand extends from the lower arm in a straight line.

Mistakes in Gripping the Spear and Javelin

1. The shaft is grasped like a club (lies in the hollow of the hand). No throwing position is possible.

2. The hand does not extend from the lower arm. (The javelin is held at too steep or at too much of an angle to the throwing direction.)

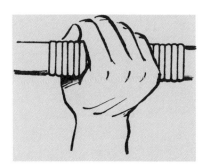
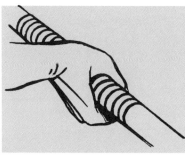

1 ---and

Important Points for the Run-up and Delivery Preparation (Right-Handed Throwers)

For Rounders Throwing

1. The run-up consists of 3 to 5 strides.

2. The throwing arm is extended back from the beginning. Count "Left—and-Throw!," with 5 strides: "1—2—3—and—throw!"

For Club and Javelin Throwing

1. The run-up: 4 to 6 strides increase the pace; a five-stride rhythm prepares for the throw.

2. Bring the throwing arm back in a straight line on "1—2—3—" of the five-stride rhythm.

1... 2... 3... and

Important Points for the Impulse Stride

- The impulse stride is the second last stride of the run-up. It is made with the right foot and it brings you into throwing position. It is the most important part of the run-up.

- The impulse stride is the same for all forms of throwing. The throwing hand remains behind the trunk at this time in order to reach as far back as possible.

- The right leg is flat during this stride and brought forward quickly. The toes point slightly outward.

- The upper body rotates almost 90° to the right. The trunk leans back.

- The pelvis does not rotate as far as the upper body, resulting in a twisted position.

- The throw is started with the last stride (left leg forward). Do not hop on the right leg before making the throw.

M1

Peter reaches back well, but:
His pelvis ....
His right foot ....
In this position he will not make a good transition to the throw. He will have to add an unnecessary hop which will ruin the run up.

M2

This is a good impulse stride, but:
Peter's throwing arm......................
By doing this, he wastes the arm strength that is so necessary for a good throw. Explain to him what he's doing wrong and show him the proper position.

M3

David is rigid, because:
His throwing arm ....
....
In this position, the back cannot be arched. He thus throws with his arm only and not his entire body.

M4

A frequent throwing mistake.
David's head ....
His upper body ....
Usually this is the result of an improper arm movement. (M3). The object thrown will not accelerate in a straight line and will fly too flat.

Pay Attention to the Delivery

- The throw begins as soon as the body is over the right leg.

- The throw is initiated by the extension of the right leg, the rapid forward movement of the right shoulder, the upward rotation of the elbow of the throwing arm, and the supportive planting of the slightly bent left leg in front of the body.

- The back arches like a whip that is lashed forward. The arch is greatest between the upper arm, shoulder and upper body.

- The throwing arm whips forward out of this arching. The body weight shifts onto the left leg that is now also extended. The right foot should remain touching the ground even if only with the toes. This leaves behind dragging prints. After the throw, fall back on your right leg.

M5

Paul uses his trunk well, but:
His left leg ....
Because of this he bends too sharply at the hips and will be low at the moment of delivery. The strength of the left leg is not used in the throw.

M6

Michael makes a serious mistake!
His right leg ....
The natural strength is totally hindered. The cause lies mostly with the reaching back of the throwing arm.

Illustrated Summary Table of Mistakes

Mistake	Illustration
Grip mistakes 1 and 2: Ball is held too tightly or too loosely.	
Grip mistakes 3 and 4: Javelin gripped like a club. Wrist bends downward.	
M1 Pelvis and right foot turned too much to the right.	
M2 Throwing arm not extended.	
M3 Throwing arm is too much to the side of the body.	
M4 Head and body tend toward the left during the delivery.	
M5 Left leg is too far forward, so the thrower bends at the hips.	
M6 The right leg is forward — no normal transition of strength is possible.	

Correction of Mistakes and Choice of Exercises

Correction	Exercise
Look closely at the picture and explanation of the grip. Practise the proper grip.	No special exercise.
Look closely at the picture and explanation of the grip. Practise the grip. Always bend the throwing hand.	No special exercise.
Try to place toes firmly forward and twist the hips.	G: — S: T3, exercises 1 and 2; T4, exercise 7.
Bring arm firmly back. Throw often from a standing position.	G: — S: T3, all exercises with extended arm; T4, all exercises.
Stretching and mobility exercises for the shoulders; target throws over the head.	G: all loosening exercises for throwing, p. 111-115. S: T1 and T2, all exercises.
Throw over high obstacles, follow the flight path with your eyes.	G: — S: T1 and T3, all exercises.
Throw with the delivery stride in which the left leg is placed from above and then extended.	G: — S. T3, especially variant 1.
Begin delivery rhythm with left foot — practise slowly and count off carefully.	G: loosening exercises (a) and (b) on p. 111. .S: T3 and T4, all exercises.

Preparing for the Throw

Where to Throw

Only throw in areas where you cannot cause any damage to plants or buildings (fruit trees, lights, windows, doors, cars) and where you cannot hit or injure anyone.

Athletes should be disciplined and pay attention to safety regulations whenever they throw. Whenever possible use only sports fields, large playgrounds, stubble fields and other open areas where your throwing path is open and unobstructed.

Throwing against slopes has the advantage that the object cannot fly far and that the ball and club roll part of the way back (making retrieval easier).

What to Throw

Suitable objects are:

1. Pieces of wood and branches up to arm thickness and approximately 30 to 50 cm long, in place of a club.

2. Stones approximately the size of a fist. They are easily found in sandy soil or gravel pits.

3. Handy hard rubber balls (e.g. field hockey balls).

4. Small metal balls weighing no more than 1 kg.

5. 1.5 to 2 m-long sticks or poles can be used as spears and thrown like a javelin.

How to Train

As in other disciplines, the training program depends on the physical characteristics most needed for ball, club, and javelin throwing. Sports researchers and trainers have determined that throwing skill, and therefore the technique and the speed of the throwing arm, are even more important than strength.

In addition, the mobility of the shoulders is very important, so that the back can be properly arched. Your training must be based on the following rules:

1. Throw often; always use the same strength, because only in so doing can you develop a "fast arm."

2. Throw different objects. The frequent change of object greatly influences throwing skill.

3. Throw from different starting positions, but especially from a run. This also develops throwing skill.

4. The throwing of heavy objects serves primarily to train strength. It should only make up about one-third of the training.

5. Throwing with the weaker arm is also very useful. Hold competitions in which you throw with both your right and left arm. Add the distances reached together!

6. Do not leave warm-up exercises out of any training session.

Determine your performance level at the beginning of training. Write down the first score in your exercise book and set a goal of increasing your performance level under the motto: throw often!

Table 4 Throwing performance norms for youth.

	Performance (in m)		
	Poor Girls Boys (under)	Intermediate Girls Boys (around)	Good Girls Boys (over)
Youth B	15 26 17 29	19 31 22 34	30 50
Youth A	18 26 20 29	24 35 26 40	20 28 (Javelin, 600g)

T1 Two-Handed Throwing Over the Head

For these you need a heavy object. Medicine balls are best. But you can also use large pieces of wood, large bricks and home-made sandbags. You must practise so that both arms are used effectively in throwing. Two-handed throwing forces you to throw over your head. At the same time, you will feel how the upper body and the legs work together. Pay attention to the following:

1. Throw from the stride position (left leg forward) or from an impulse stride (left leg forward and throw).

2. In the starting position, or after the impulse stride, the body weight is on the right leg, the body leans far backward.

3. The object is behind the head; the hands are cupped behind it.

4. The elbow must be pushed firmly forward.

5. In the throw, first the right leg extends, then the left.

6. The upper body moves forward energetically out of a back arch.

1. **Distance throwing over a high obstacle.**
   8 to 10 times
   As an obstacle, stretch a piece of elastic approximately 2 m high or use the goal on the sports field. Try to move the throwing line further and further away from the obstacle.

2. **As in exercise 1, but with an impulse stride.**
   8 to 10 times

3. **Bounce the ball against the wall.**
   10 to 12 times
   Stand far enough away from the wall that you can catch the bouncing ball. Throw hard enough that you can move farther away from

the wall. Remember that the wall should not be damaged. Only medicine balls are suitable.

4. **Ball throwing in pairs.**
   Throw until one partner wins. Always throw from where the object has landed. The winner is the one who throws past the line that lies approximately 10 m behind each competitor.

Flexibility Exercises:
a. Describe circles with your arms (right arm backwards, left arm forwards).
b. Whip arms from a crossed-arm to a back position.

T2 Throwing from Different Starting Positions

Throw from all positions with the proper arm movement above the shoulder and the head. This will improve both your throwing technique and your distance.

Pay attention:

1. The elbow remains close to the head when reaching back. The lower arm hangs loosely down behind the head.

2. The arm movement must follow a straight line past the head. It is easy to know if this is the case when throwing a club or similar implement. You can tell from the flight path whether the arm followed a straight line; if the object turns on an angle in the air, you know that the arm movement was not straight.

3. The right shoulder and the upper body lead the throw through a strong forward pull.

1. **Target throwing from a sitting or kneeling position.**
   15 to 20 throws
   Alternate throwing clubs, pieces of wood, stones, and rounders. For targets use tree trunks, bicycle tires, or use goals made of sticks set closer and closer together. You will notice how difficult it is to score with each different object one after the other. Count how often in a row you hit the target. Keep moving farther away from the target. It is important that you can still hit the target from a distance.

2. **Target throwing for concealed targets.**
   20 to 30 throws

The targets must be made so that you can hear a hit (old pails are good).

3. **Target throws from a sitting position over high obstacles.**
   15 to 20 throws
   Throw over hedges and trees.

Flexibility Exercises:
a. Stretching the shoulder muscles.
b. Practising the back arch. Grip the door handle with the lower arm turned up, right shoulder forward, elbow up and right leg extended.

T3 Throwing from the Stride Position and with the Impulse Stride

With these throws, we come considerably closer to the proper technique. Throw clubs, iron balls, or heavy stones. If you can, carve yourselves spears. The important thing in practising is to throw as far as possible, to train the "fast arm."

Pay attention:

1. Do not draw your arm back yet. Instead, leave the elbow forward by the head, as shown in the picture.

2. Before the throw, the body weight rests on the slightly bent right leg.

3. Try to use the whole body in the delivery. However, you must not lean from the hips. Remain as straight as possible.

4. Step forward with your right foot, as soon as you have thrown and you do not fall forward.

> **Attention!**
> Pay special attention to safety when throwing heavy objects.
> Do not throw unless you are absolutely certain no one is anywhere near your throwing field.

Here are two other technical variations:

1. **Throwing with one stride.**

   The starting position is slightly unusual, because the right leg is forward. You go into the familiar delivery position, but when the left leg is brought forward to initiate it. The stride is what is special in this exercise. You should feel how the legs extend, one after the other.

2. **Throwing with the impulse stride.**

   The starting position is the same as the standing throw; however, before the delivery, you make the springy, flat impulse stride with the right leg, which leads immediately into the delivery. The throw has two strides, since the left leg steps forward at the end.

Flexibility Exercises:
a. Grip the javelin or spear with hands a little more than shoulder-width apart and swing it over the head to the buttocks and back.
b. Push the spear or javelin against a tree or wall, and arch the back through a forward step to the left.

Left —　　and　　throw

T4 Throwing from a Run

Running and throwing — they must flow smoothly into each other without pausing. Many pupils have problems with this. You should simply throw often from a run. Do not worry if you do not reach back properly at first. What is important is that right-handed throwers have the left foot forward for a delivery.

As soon as you feel surer of yourself, practise the reaching back movement as well. With light objects, bring your arm back on the second last stride, like the girl in the picture. Then count: "left—and—throw!"

If you are throwing heavy objects, clubs, spears or javelins, bring the arm back before you run up.

Only after you have learned the five-stride rhythm, can you use it during these throws. Until you have learned it properly, the hesitation of bringing back your arm before the throw is certain to disturb the flow of the run-up. Avoid this as much as possible.

Always strive to hit the farthest possible target when you throw.

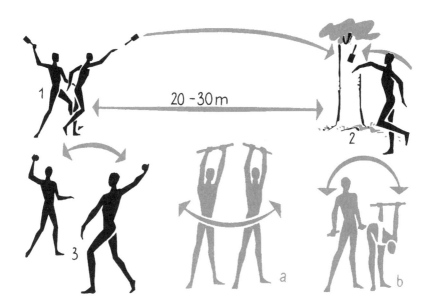

1. **Target throwing in the running direction.**
   15 to 20 times
   At first use wide targets and then make them narrower. Increase the distance as well.

2. **Target throwing at side targets when running by.**
   15 to 20 times
   Who can hit the target running the fastest?

3. **Throwing at moving targets.**
   15 to 20 times
   With soft rubber balls or, in winter, with snow balls, you can practise with a partner. Run by each other 15 to 20 m away and try to hit each other.

4. **Distance throwing from a run.**
   15 to 20 times

Set up some targets and try to hit them.

5. **Distance throwing with the spear and javelin.**
   15 to 20 times
   One person begins. The others try to throw their spears so that they land close to the first. Who can come the closest?

Flexibility Exercises

a. Stand in a straddle position and rotate the trunk, holding the javelin high in the air, hands shoulder-width apart.

b. Stand in a straddle position, bend trunk and swing arms up and back while holding object.

10 - 15 m

1. Bounce target throwing.

This game is for 2 to 6 players. An open place in front of a flat wall can provide a playing field. Each player needs a tennis or rubber ball and 4 to 6 clubs or wooden sticks of the same size that can be stuck into the ground.

Each player lines up his clubs in front of the wall about 4 to 5 m away. From a throwing line, the players take turns throwing the balls against the wall so that they bounce back and knock over the opponent's clubs. The winner is the one who knocks over all the clubs first.

2. "Running the gauntlet" with defensive throwing.

A game for winter. Some throwers stand 2 to 3 m apart on a line. They prepare 3 or 4 loosely packed snow balls (hard balls are dangerous). One person runs along a line 10 to 15 m away and also takes 3 or 4 snow balls with him. The throwers try to hit the runner as often as possible. He or she, in turn, tries to avoid the balls by dodging and through interference throwing.

The winner is the one who is hit least while running.

Shot-Putting

More Strength—Better Performance.

Muscular strength, along with speed, is important for good performance in most track and field events. In shot putting it is the decisive factor. The more you practise with the shot, the more you muscles will adapt and, of course, the more strength you will have.

One former shot putter, now a sports researcher, gives this advice:

"I trained enthusiastically while I was a kid. I trained in many areas, played handball, swam, and practised track and field. In the multidiscipline event, I was especially successful. I ran the 80 m hurdles in 12.2 s, high jumped 1.48 m, long jumped 5.38 m and put the shot 14.85 m. All this required lots of practice. I acquired my strength first through shot putting. The shot is very important event, especially for children, since nearly all the muscles of the body are used and developed. As they become stronger you will be able to handle the shot much more easily. All young track and field athletes should shot put, not matter what their specialty. It's hard at first. But if you practise shot putting long and hard, your performance in all track and field events will improve.

A lot of girls think it's too difficult for them. It will be, as long as you're untrained. I was bad at the start.—I managed 7.05 m when I was 13. But a few years later my hard training was rewarded with a youth record: 14.85 m. Performance can improve if you train hard."

Technique and Training for Shot-Putting

The put is the most important factor.

In shot putting you must put from a relatively small putting circle with a radius of 2.135 m. So there isn't much room for the whole movement. It has 4 phases known as the "initial position," "glide," "put," and "recovery." The "initial position" can be compared to reaching back in throwing, and the "glide" to the run-up, which helps you build up the highest possible speed in the putting direction in limited space. To take full advantage of the radius, we begin the put with our backs to the putting direction, we can then bend forward in the "initial position." The body has more freedom of movement in this direction than bending to the side. Pupils should begin with their backs to the stop board in the so-called standing put as well, which is made without the complicated glide movement, even when this starting position is uncomfortable. For young people, the standing put is the most important practice and training form, because the put, by far the most effective phase, is learned with it. For this reason you only find the standing put in the exercise section. Here also, you should hold a small competition once a month to check your strength growth. Compare your distance to norms in the table below.

Table 5 Shot-putting performance norms for youth

	Performance (in m)					
	Poor Girls Boys (under)		Intermediate Girls Boys (around)		Good Girls Boys (over)	
Youth B	4.00 4.50 (3 kg) 4.50 5.00		4.50 5.50 (3 kg) 5.00 6.00		6.00 7.50 (3 kg) (4 kg)	
Youth A	4.80 5.00 (3 kg) (3 kg) 5.00 4.60 (3 kg) (4 kg)		5.50 6.75 (3 kg) (3 kg) 6.00 6.00 (3 kg) (4 kg)		7.00 9.00 (3 KG) (4 KG)	

How to hold the shot:

- The shot rests on the base of the fingers in the shot hand.
- The middle fingers are spread a little, the thumb and baby finger support the shot from the sides.
- With this hold, the shot is pressed against the neck beside the chin.

Mistakes in holding the shot:

- The shot rests too far off the shoulder. Because of this, the elbow is not right under the shot.
- The shot does not rest on the base of the fingers but in the palm of hand. There is no contact with the neck.

M1

M2

Important points for the initial position:

- Begin in an upright position on the right leg with your back to the putting direction.

- For the initial position, bend the trunk forward and bring the swinging leg back and up for balance.

- Then bend the standing leg and bring the swinging leg back.

Mistakes in the initial position:

- The starting position is not with the back to the putting direction but sideways.

- The swinging leg moves by the standing leg at the end of the initial position, creating a poor center of gravity for the glide.

M3

M4

M5

Ann illustrates a very common beginners' mistake:
Her swinging leg ....
....
The result is not enough energy to glide the two-foot length needed.

M6

The swinging leg is too high.
Can you think what the result will be?
The glide will ....
This goes against the principle of having the path of momentum as straight as possible.

Important Points for the Glide:

- It begins with an energetic but flat swing of the left leg in the direction of the stop board.

- At the same time the standing leg is straight and you move (without jumping) toward the centre of the putting circle.

- In doing this, push down with the sole of the foot. The right foot glides along the ground and is pulled to the centre of the circle under the body.

- As the foot and knee swing toward the putting direction (foot at 120°, knee up to 90° to the putting direction), the upper body remains unchanged, with the back to putting direction.

- The swinging leg quickly lowers after the swing, fully extended down so that the foot is planted on the inside edge and pushes against the stop board.

- In this way, the forward movement is checked and directed upward. The put position has been reached.

M7

What is Philip doing wrong in the glide?
He is already rotating his upper body
. ...
Show him his mistake and give him a tip so he can avoid the problem in the future.

M8

How did Katherine get into this poor putting position?
During the glide, her standing leg did not sufficiently ....
Because of this her body weight is already on the left leg.

M9

Claudia wants to put the shot very quickly, but:
Her upper body ....
while her legs and right hip still have not rotated and are not extended. In this position she loses valuable strength.

M10

Paula wants to put the shot very high, but:
Her entire right side ....
....
She thus leaves a considerable piece of the momentum path unused and puts sideways over her head.

Pay Attention During the Put:

- The put immediately follows the glide with an explosive extension of both legs along with the lifting and rotating of the trunk in the putting direction.

- At the beginning of the extension, the right knee and hips have swivelled in the putting direction.

- The upper body is first raised and only then is it rotated in the putting direction. But the movement should happen very rapidly.

- Only after this rotation does the putting hand leave the neck and push with full strength forward and up.

- The shot should leave the hand at the highest point possible. For this reason, the body must be fully extended at the end.

- The left side of the body forms an axis and the body rotates around it, remaining upright.

M11

Andrew does not use his strength and body height, since:
His hips ....
His legs . ...
Compare his put position with the ideal described on page 126. Demonstrate him his mistake.

M12

Look especially closely at this picture! Stephen throws the shot because his elbow is not . ...
....
Therefore it is not possible for him to transfer the strength in his legs and trunk to the shot.

Illustrated Table of Mistakes

Mistake	Illustration

M1 Shot and elbow are too far to the right.

M2 Shot is cupped in the hand, not laid against the shoulder and neck.

M3 Side starting position—back is not in the putting direction.

M4 Foot of the swinging leg swings through—unfavourable centre of gravity.

M5 Weak use of swinging leg.

M6 Swinging leg is too high—leads to a jump.

M7 Upper body is already rotating toward the putting direction in the glide.

M8 Left leg pushes down too late—body weight is already on the left.

M9 The put is initiated by the trunk. rotation—the legs are not used.

M10 Put is sideways over the head becausethe right side has not swivelled far enough forward.

M11 Bending at the hips—low put, flat flight curve of the shot.

M12 Elbow is not behind but under the shot—this is a throw.

Correction of Mistakes and Choice of Exercise

Correction	Exercises
Hold shot to the neck on the collarbone.	No special exercise— always concentrate before the put!
Pay attention to the proper position of the shot before the put.	No special exercise—learn the position on p. 122.
Practise starting position keeping back in putting direction.	Look at proper position on p. 123 once more.
Lower foot when it swings back until it just lightly touches the ground.	No special exercise— always concentrate!
Initiate the glide only through the swinging leg.	G: 3 to 5, p.14. S: no special exercise.
Use swinging leg in direction of the stop board.	No special exercise—pay attention to proper use.
Keep looking at the back end of the circle in the glide.	No special exercise—look at an orientation point.
Push down by planting left leg quickly and actively.	G: — S: SP 1, exercise 3; SP 3.
First straighten the trunk, and only then consciously rotate.	G: 1, 2, and 5, p. 14. S: SP 2 and SP 3, all exercises.
Rotate entire side of body forward, especially the chest.	G: 3 and 4, p.15. S: SP 3.
Take-off during the put without changing foot position.	G: 1 and 4, p.13. S: SP 1, all exercises.
Push elbow outward, finger tips inward.	G: 1, 2, and 4, p.15. S: SP 1 and SP 3, all exercises.

SP 1 Two-Handed Shot Putting Exercises

For these and the following exercises, you should use heavy objects. If you do not have proper shots, use heavy medicine balls, large stones, old bowling balls, or even bricks. When choosing a place to practise, remember the tips we listed on page 108. For best results, put against a slope or an embankment so the shot can roll back. Make sure that no one walks into the target area while you are throwing.

Pay attention to the following technical points:

1. In the starting position, have both hands behind the object with the finger tips together, and the object held against the chest.

2. Elbows should be out and the lower arm approximately horizontal.

3. Initially bend the knees lightly in practising; as your skill increases, use stronger bends in order to use the extension strength of both legs in every put.

4. Put high rather than far, so that your body can be fully extended.

1. **Putting to each other.**
   8 to 12 times
   Do this only with medicine balls. The partners must try to put the ball to each other from the greatest possible distance.

2. **Put over a high obstacle from a crouch.**
   8 to 10 times
   The obstacle might be either a piece of elastic stretched at a height of approximately 2 m or a soccer goal. Extend the body fully during the put so that it leads to a slight jump. The higher you put, the more effective it is.

3. **Putting from a stride position.**
   8 to 12 times

In the initial position, the back leg is bent and the weight rests on it.

4. **Putting from a sitting position.**
   8 to 12 times
   The trunk leans slightly backward to begin and pushes forward and up.

Flexibility Exercises:

a. Sweeping circles with the trunk and arms.
b. Lower leg circles, left and right.

SP 2 Throwing Backward over the Head

You probably are wondering how such throws could be good training for shot putting. Let us to explain.

Because the put starts with the putter's back to the putting direction, we are able not only to reach much farther back, but also to use the back muscles for the put. They are the longest muscles of the body and they represent an important reserve of strength that can produce high speed for the shot. They are used to lift the upper body quickly at the beginning of the put. But only when these muscles are strong enough can you take good advantage of them.

Technically, these throws are simple, but you should take the fol-

lowing points into consideration.

● Since several very strong muscles are being used at the same time, the objects to be thrown should be as heavy as possible. Medicine balls are particularly suitable and relatively safe. The safety factor is important since you cannot see where you are throwing during the throw.

● Swing the object through from between the legs and reach back as far as possible, so that the muscles are stretched well forward.

● Throw the object so that it travels in a high arch.

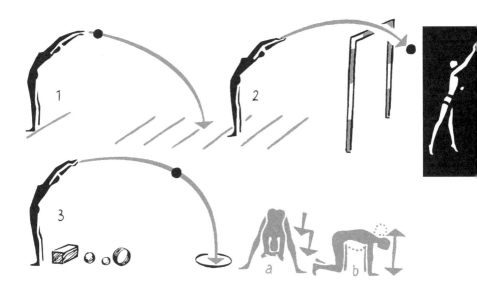

1. Zone throwing.
6 to 8 times

From a mark, try to hit the furthest zone possible. The distance of first zone is determined according to the weight of the object being thrown.

2. Zone throwing over a high obstacle.
6 to 8 times

The object should go over the obstacle (such as a goal). Try to move back a zone after every successful throw.

3. Target throwing.
6 times

Select a distance at which you can just throw the heaviest object to the target circle with great exertion! Attempt to throw all the objects (stones of different weights, medicine ball, sand bag, etc.) into the circle from this distance.

Flexibility Exercises:

a. Bend the trunk forward with crossed arms, touch elbows to the ground.

b. On hands and knees—alternately hollow your back and arch like a cat.

SP 3   One-Handed Shot Putting Exercises

In contrast to two-handed putting, in this exercise only the putting hand is behind the object which rests on the right shoulder, while the other hand provides support from the side or front:

There are two basic forms for this put:

a. From a front position, with the chest in the putting direction; with the feet level and slightly apart. In the initial position, the knees are slightly bent, but the right shoulder does not lean backward.

b. Take up the putting position that is reached after the glide (see p.124). The back should therefore be in the putting direction, but the right foot and the right hip are swivelled almost 90°.

When using a large object, such as a medicine ball, the left hand holds it above, to hold the ball in the right position against the putting hand. During the put itself, the right hand should remain behind the object.

All the variations shown on pages 131 and 133 are suitable exercises.

Check Your Progress

Plan Your Progress and Determine Your Results

The purpose of this book is to help you achieve good or even very good performance levels. Whatever your ultimate goal in sports—whatever motivates you to get involved—you must train regularly to succeed. Intentions are sometimes not good enough. Keep a diary, a "training book," to record your progress. Record your training progress accurately. Every serious athlete has a training book.

In the first half of the book, record the day, length of training session, the program and level of exertion (see table below for sample recordings). In the second half, set up a performance graph, as illustrated on the next page. By using different colors for performance points and lines, you can put several disciplines on one graph and see everything at a glance. For example:

red = 60 m race
green = endurance run
blue = rounders throw, etc.

If you don't have enough colours, the connecting lines can be drawn in different ways (dots, dashes, dots and dashes, etc.).

The point values are found in the tables on the following pages.

The resulting curves show you whether you are training hard enough, and what disciplines you should train harder in!

Sample page from a training diary

Date	Length of session	Program	Results
5.9	60 min.	Circuit training Sprint S 1 and S 2	very strenous, legs heavy
8.9	50 min.	Endurance running	heavy sweating, became slower at end
12.9	75 min.	Sprint S 2 Shot put SP 1,2	fresh; throwing object somewhat too light

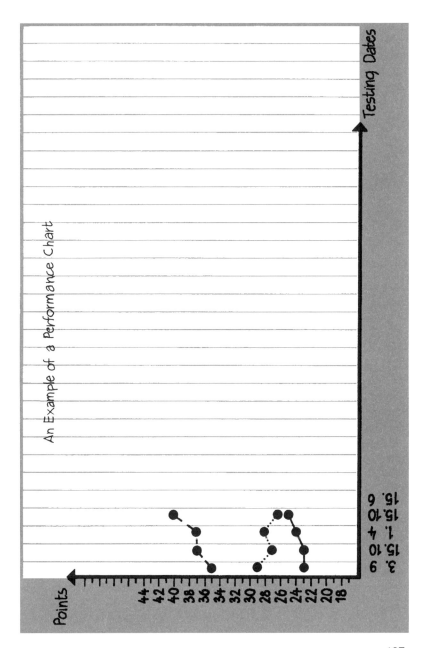

An Example of a Performance Chart

Performance norms for girls

Points	60 m	Distance	Height	Ball	400m 600m	60 m	Distance	Height	Ball	600 m 800 m
46	10,5	3,12	—	26,02	1:00,7	—	3,51	1,03	31,25	1:30,1
45	—	3,09	0,92	25,58	1:01,1	—	3,48	1,02	30,75	1:30,5
44	10,6	3,06	0,91	25,15	1:01,6	10,0	3,45	1,01	30,25	1:30,9
43	—	3,03	0,90	24,72	1:02,0	—	3,42	1,00	29,75	1:31,3
42	—	3,00	0,89	24,28	1:02,4	10,1	3,39	—	29,00	1:31,7
41	10,7	2,97	0,88	23.85	1:02,8	—	3,37	0,99	28,50	1:32,1
40	—	2,94	0,87	23,42	1:03,2	10,2	3,34	0,98	28,00	1:32,5
39	10,8	2,90	0,86	22,68	1:04,0	—	3,29	0,97	27,50	1:33,2
38	10,9	2,85	0,85	21,94	1:04,7	10,3	3,24	0,95	26,75	1:33,9
37	11,0	2,80	0,83	21,20	1:05,4	10,4	3,19	0,94	26,00	1:34,6
36	11,1	2,75	0,82	20,45	1:06,1	10,5	3,14	0,92	25,50	1:35,3
35	11,2	2,70	0,80	19,71	1:06,8	—	3,09	0,91	24,75	1:36,0
34	11,3	2,65	0,79	18,97	1:07,5	10,6	3,04	0,90	24,00	1:36,7
33	—	2,60	0,77	18,23	1:08,3	10,7	2,99	0,88	23,50	1:37,4
32	11,4	2,55	0,76	17,49	1:09,0	10,8	2,94	0,87	22,75	1:38,1
31	11,5	2,50	0,74	16,75	1:09,7	—	2,89	0,85	22,25	1:38,8
30	11,6	2,45	0,73	16,01	1:10,4	—	2,84	0,84	21,50	1:39,5
29	11,7	2,40	0,72	15,27	1:11,1	11,0	2,79	0,83	20,75	1:40,2
28	11,8	2,35	0,70	14,53	1:11,8	—	2,74	0,81	20,25	1:40,9
27	11,9	2,30	0,69	13,79	1:12,6	11,1	2,69	0,80	19,50	1:41,5
26	—	2,25	0,67	13,05	1:13,3	11,2	2,64	0,78	18,75	1:42,2
25	12,0	2,20	0,66	12,31	1:14,0	11,3	2,59	0,77	18,25	1:42,9
24	12,1	2,15	0,64	11,57	1:14,7	—	2,54	0,76	17,50	1:43,6
23	12,2	2,11	0,63	10,83	1:15,4	11,4	2,49	0,75	17,00	1:44,3
22	12,3	2,09	0,61	10,09	1:16,1	11,5	2,44	0,73	16,25	1:45,0
21	12,4	2,01	0,59	9,34	1:16,9	11,6	2,39	0,71	15,50	1:45,7
20	12,5	1,96	0,58	9,60	1:17,6	11,7	2,34	0,70	15,00	1:46,4
19	—	1,91	0,57	8,20	1:18,3	—	2,29	0,69	14,25	1:47,1
18	12,6	1,86	0,56	7,79	1:19,0	11,8	2,24	0,67	13,75	1:47,8
46	10,2	3,31	0,98	27,50	1:31,9	—	3,74	1,13	7,72	1:46,6
45	—	3,29	—	27,25	1:32,3	9,8	3,71	1,12	7,63	1:47,2
44	10,3	3,26	0,97	26,75	1:32,7	—	3,68	—	7,54	1:47,7
43	—	3,23	0,96	26,25	1:33,1	9,9	3,66	1,11	7,45	1:48,2
42	10,4	3,20	0,95	25,75	1:33,5	—	3,63	1,10	7,36	1:48,7
41	—	3,17	0,94	25,25	1:33,9	10,0	3,60	1,09	7,25	1:49,2
40	—	3,15	0,93	24,75	1:34,3	—	3,57	1,08	7,17	1:49,7
39	10,5	3,10	0,92	24,25	1:35,0	10,1	3,52	1,07	7,01	1:50,6
38	10,6	3,05	0,91	23,75	1:35,7	10,2	3,47	1,05	7,85	1:51,4
37	10,7	3,00	0,90	23,00	1:36,4	10,3	3,42	1,04	6,70	1:52,3
36	—	2,96	0,88	22,50	1:37,1	—	3,37	1,02	6,54	1:53,2
35	10,8	2,91	0,87	22,00	1:37,8	10,4	3,31	1,01	6,38	1:54,1
34	10,9	2,86	0,86	21,25	1:38,5	—	3,26	1,00	6,22	1:54,9
33	11,0	2,82	0,84	20,75	1:39,2	10,5	3,21	0,98	6,06	1:55,8
32	—	2,77	0,83	20,25	1:39,9	—	3,16	0,97	5,91	1:56,7
31	11,1	2,72	0,82	19,50	1:40,6	10,6	3,11	0,95	5,75	1:57,5
30	11,2	2,67	0,80	19,00	1:41,3	10,7	3,06	0,94	5,59	1:58,4
29	11,3	2,63	0,79	18,50	1:42,0	10,8	3,01	0,92	5,43	1:59,3
28	11,4	2,58	0,77	17,75	1:42,7	—	2,96	0,91	5,27	2:00,1
27	—	2,53	0,76	17,25	1:43,3	10,9	2,91	0,90	5,12	2:01,0
26	11,5	2,48	0,75	16,50	1:44,0	11,0	2,86	0,88	4,96	2:01,9
25	11,6	2,44	0,73	16,00	1:44,7	11,1	2,81	0,87	4,80	2:02,8
24	11,7	2,39	0,72	15,50	1:45,4	—	2,76	0,85	4,64	2:03,6
23	—	2,34	0,71	14,75	1:46,1	11,2	2,71	0,84	4,48	2:04,5
22	11,8	2,29	0,69	14,25	1:46,8	11,3	2,66	0,82	4,33	2:05,4
21	11,9	2,25	0,68	13,75	1:47,5	11,4	2,61	0,81	4,17	2:06,2
20	12,0	2,20	0,67	13,00	1:48,2	11,5	2,56	0,80	4,01	2:07,1
19	12,1	2,15	0,65	12,50	1:48,9	—	2,51	0,78	3,85	2:08,0
18	—	2,10	0,64	12,00	1:49,6	11,6	2,46	0,77	3,69	2:08,8

Performance norms for boys

Points	60 m	Distance	Height	Ball	400 m 600 m	60 m	Distance	Height	Ball	600 m 800 m
46	9,9	3,45	1,01	38,68	1:20,9	—	3,81	—	47,50	2:18,4
45	—	3,42	—	38,21	1:21,4	—	3,78	1,11	47,00	2:19,0
44	10,0	3,39	1,00	37,75	1:21,9	9,7	3,75	1,10	46,25	2:19,7
43	—	3,36	0,99	37,28	1:22,4	—	3,71	1,09	45,75	2:20,3
42	—	3,33	0,98	36,81	1:22,9	9,8	3,68	1,08	45,25	2:20,9
41	10,1	3,30	0,97	36,34	1:23,3	—	3,65	1,07	44,50	2:21,5
40	—	3,27	0,96	36,88	1:23,8	9,9	3,62	1,06	44,00	2:22,1
39	10,2	3,22	0,95	35,08	1:24,7	—	3,57	1,05	43,00	2:23,2
38	10,3	3,17	0,93	34,28	1:25,5	10,0	3,52	1,03	42,00	2:24,2
37	10,4	3,12	0,92	33,48	1:26,3	10,1	3,47	1,02	41,00	2:25,2
36	—	3,07	0,90	32,68	1:27,2	10,2	3,41	1,01	40,00	2:26,4
35	10,5	3,02	0,89	31,88	1:28,0	—	3,36	0,99	39,00	2:27,4
34	10,6	2,97	0,87	31,08	1:28,8	10,3	3,31	0,98	38,25	2:28,5
33	10,7	2,92	0,86	30,28	1:29,7	10,4	3,26	0,96	37,25	2:29,5
32	—	2,87	0,84	29,49	1:30,5	10,5	3,21	0,95	36,25	2:30,6
31	10,8	2,82	0,83	28,69	1:31,3	—	3,15	0,93	35,25	2:31,7
30	10,9	2,77	0,81	27,89	1:32,2	10,6	3,10	0,92	34,25	2:32,7
29	11,0	2,72	0,79	27,09	1:33,0	10,7	3,05	0,90	33,25	2:33,8
28	11,1	2,67	0,78	26,29	1:33,8	—	3,00	0,89	32,25	2:34,8
27	—	2,62	0,76	25,49	1:34,7	10,8	2,95	0,87	31,25	2:35,9
26	11,2	2,57	0,75	24,69	1:35,5	10,9	2,89	0,86	30,25	2:37,0
25	11,3	2,52	0,73	23,89	1:36,3	11,0	2,85	0,84	29,25	2:39,0
24	11,4	2,47	0,72	23,09	1:37,2	—	2,79	0,83	28,25	2:39,1
23	—	2,42	0,70	22,30	1:38,0	11,1	2,74	0,82	27,25	2:40,1
22	11,5	2,37	0,69	21,50	1:38,8	11,2	2,69	0,80	26,25	2:41,2
21	11,6	2,32	0,67	20,70	1:39,7	11,3	2,63	0,79	25,25	2:42,3
20	11,7	2,27	0,66	19,90	1:40,5	—	2,58	0,77	24,50	2:43,3
19	—	2,22	0,64	19,10	1:41,3	11,4	2,53	0,76	23,50	2:44,4
18	11,8	2,16	0,63	18,30	1:42,2	11,5	2,48	0,75	22,50	2:45,5
46	—	3,70	1,07	42,75	2:21,3	—	4,05	1,21	7,64	2:54,5
45	—	3,67	1,06	42,25	2:21,9	—	4,02	1,20	7,54	2:55,3
44	9,9	3,64	—	41,75	2:22,5	9,5	3,99	1,19	7,44	2:56,1
43	—	3,61	1,05	41,25	2:23,1	—	3,96	1,18	7,34	2:56,9
42	10,0	3,58	1,04	40,75	2:23,8	9,6	3,92	1,17	7,25	2:57,7
41	—	3,55	1,03	40,25	2:24,4	—	3,89	—	7,15	2:58,6
40	—	3,52	1,02	39,75	2:25,0	9,7	3,86	1,16	7,05	2:59,4
39	10,1	3,47	1,01	38,75	2:26,0	—	3,80	1,14	6,89	3:00,8
38	10,2	3,42	0,99	38,00	2:27,1	9,8	3,75	1,12	6,72	3:02,2
37	10,3	3,37	0,98	37,00	2:28,2	9,9	3,70	1,11	6,55	3:03,6
36	10,4	3,32	0,96	36,25	2:29,2	10,0	3,64	1,09	6,39	3:05,0
35	—	3,27	0,95	35,25	2:30,3	—	3,59	1,08	6,22	3:06,4
34	10,5	3,22	0,94	34,50	2:31,3	10,1	3,53	1,06	6,05	3:07,9
33	10,6	3,17	0,92	33,50	2:32,4	10,2	3,48	1,05	5,89	3:09,3
32	10,7	3,12	0,91	32,50	2:33,5	10,3	3,42	1,03	5,72	3:10,7
31	—	3,07	0,89	31,75	2:34,5	—	3,37	1,02	5,56	3:12,1
30	10,8	3,02	0,88	31,00	2:35,6	10,4	3,31	1,00	5,39	3:13,5
29	10,9	2,97	0,86	30,00	2:36,6	10,5	3,26	0,98	5,22	3:14,0
28	—	2,92	0,85	29,25	2:37,7	—	3,21	0,97	5,06	3:16,3
27	11,0	2,87	0,84	28,25	2:38,8	10,6	3,15	0,95	4,89	3:17,7
26	11,1	2,82	0,82	27,50	2:39,8	10,7	3,10	0,94	4,72	3:19,1
25	11,2	2,77	0,81	26,50	2:40,9	10,8	3,04	0,92	4,56	3:20,6
24	—	2,72	0,79	25,50	2:41,9	—	2,99	0,91	4,39	3:22,0
23	11,3	2,67	0,78	24,75	2:43,0	10,9	2,93	0,89	4,22	3:23,4
22	11,4	2,62	0,76	23,75	2:44,1	11,0	2,88	0,87	4,06	3:24,8
21	11,5	2,57	0,75	23,00	2:45,1	11,1	2,82	0,86	3,89	3:26,2
20	—	2,52	0,74	22,00	2:46,2	—	2,77	0,84	3,73	3:27,6
19	11,6	2,47	0,72	21,25	2:47,2	11,2	2,72	0,83	3,56	3:29,0
18	11,7	2,42	0,71	20,25	2:48,3	11,3	2,66	0,81	3,39	3:30,4

How to Prepare Domino Cards

Carefully cut out each one of the domino exercise cards and glue them onto a cardboard of same size. The back of each card can be fitted by self drawn domino exercise cards. In this way you will obtain a wider selection of exercises to be used in your circuit training program.

How to Prepare Domino Cards

Carefully cut out each one of the domino exercise cards and glue them onto a cardboard of same size. The back of each card can be fitted by self drawn domino exercise cards. In this way you will obtain a wider selection of exercises to be used in your circuit training program.

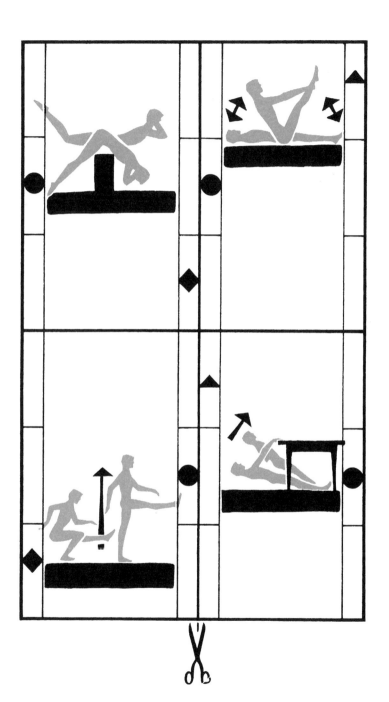